"With their complementary backgrounds, Mitchell and Riley prove to be an excellent team in their dialogue on Christian bioethics. They present valuable insights and helpful theological perspective for the newcomer to bioethics, and the seasoned ethicist will profit from it as well. A fine guide!"

Paul Copan
Professor and Pledger Family Chair of Philosophy and Ethics
Palm Beach Atlantic University

"Ben Mitchell and Joy Riley invite readers into their dialogue on profoundly important yet intensely practical issues raised in health care, medical technology, and cutting-edge research. The conversation draws on the history and practice of medicine, theological guidelines, philosophical insights, and case studies to help Christians develop awareness and wisdom about bioethical dilemmas. Riley and Mitchell demystify ethical concepts, medical terminology, and biotechnology. This highly approachable book is a noteworthy gift to Christians—laity, pastors, students, and clinicians alike."

Paige Comstock Cunningham
Executive Director
The Center for Bioethics and Human Dignity

"Though helpful to all, I particularly encourage pastors to use *Christian Bioethics: A Guide for Pastors, Health Care Professionals, and Families* to prepare their parishioners for the moral maze of today's culture. Helpful for both sermon preparation and counseling, Mitchell and Riley's practical, biblical wisdom provides guidelines for addressing common bioethical dilemmas. The church should be able to provide these answers."

Gene Rudd, M.D.
Senior Vice President
Christian Medical and Dental Associations

Christian
Bioethics

A Guide for Pastors, Health Care Professionals, and Families

B&H Studies in Biblical Ethics

Volumes Available

Taking Christian Moral Thought Seriously edited by Jeremy A. Evans
Moral Apologetics for Contemporary Christians by Mark Coppenger
Introduction to Biblical Ethics by David W. Jones
Christian Bioethics by C. Ben Mitchell and D. Joy Riley

Forthcoming Volumes

Basic Christian Ethics by Daniel R. Heimbach

B & H STUDIES IN CHRISTIAN ETHICS

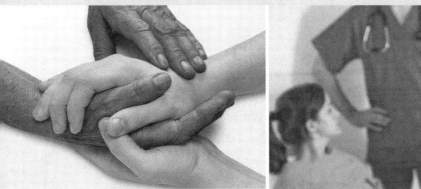

Christian
Bioethics

A Guide for Pastors, Health Care Professionals, and Families

C. BEN MITCHELL, PHD & D. JOY RILEY, MD

DANIEL R. HEIMBACH, *Series Editor*

ACADEMIC

NASHVILLE, TENNESSEE

Christian Bioethics:
A Guide for Pastors, Health Care Professionals, and Families
Copyright © 2014 by C. Ben Mitchell and D. Joy Riley

B&H Publishing Group
Nashville, Tennessee

ISBN: 978-1-4336-7114-2

Dewey Decimal Classification: 261.5
Subject Heading: BIOETHICS \ CHRISTIAN ETHICS \ MEDICAL
ETHICS

Printed in the United States of America

2 3 4 5 6 7 8 9 10 • 21 20 19 18 17

VP

In Memoriam

Edmund D. Pellegrino, MD

*A formative influence in contemporary medical ethics
who possessed an all-too-rare combination of fidelity to his faith,
brilliance in his thinking, and deep concern for humanity,
especially those who called him their physician.*

Contents

Part I: Christian Bioethics

Part II: Taking Life

Part III: Making Life

Part IV: Remaking/Faking Life

Series Preface

The greatest challenge to the life and witness of the church in our age is widespread moral confusion and denial of moral authority. This condition has been greatly influenced by a number of factors, including postmodern denial of objective truth, secularization of common life, pluralization of worldviews, and privatization of religion—all accompanied by growing hostility toward anything Christian. In fact, claims of objective moral authority and understanding are openly contested by our culture more than any other aspects of Christian faith and witness. Those who are redefining justice, character, and truth are working hard to deconstruct essential social institutions to justify a variety of ends: pursuing sensuality, elevating lifestyle over protecting innocent human life, stealing what others have fairly acquired, ridiculing the rule of law, abandoning the needy for self-fulfillment, and forsaking lifelong commitments. They reject the Judeo-Christian values on which the institutions of Western civilization were erected (i.e., marriage, property ownership, free-market enterprise, justice, law, education, and national security) and without which they cannot endure. Never in the history of the church has there been a more critical need for scholarship, instruction, and application of Christian ethics in ways that equip Christian men and women to engage the surrounding culture in prophetic moral witness.

This series aims to promote understanding and respect for the reality and relevance of God's moral truth—what Francis Schaeffer called "true truth"—in contrast to truth claims that are false or distorted. We hope these books will serve as a resource for Christians to resist compromise and to contend with the moral war raging through our culture and tormenting the church. Some authors in this series will address the interpretation of biblical teachings; others will focus on the history, theological integration, philosophical analysis, and application of Christian moral understanding. But all will use and apply God's moral truth in ways that convince the mind, convict the heart, and consume the soul.

In *Christian Bioethics: A Guide for Pastors, Health Care Professionals, and Families*, C. Ben Mitchell and D. Joy Riley introduce the field of bioethics to readers considering how Christians ought to deal with moral questions arising from circumstances faced when seeking medical treatment or possibilities generated by new advances in medical technology.

We live in an era of highly technical medicine, and while this can be comforting, it may also be confusing. How should Christians make life and death decisions? How do we move from an ancient text like the Bible to twenty-first-century questions about organ transplantation, stem-cell research, and human cloning? What kind of care do we owe one another at the end of life? Should we try to prolong life, and when should we accept mortality? Using a dialogue format, Mitchell, an ordained minister and university professor, and Riley, an experienced physician, talk openly and thoughtfully about how they as Christians think about a range of thorny ethical issues arising in their field of bioethics.

Combining their backgrounds in theology, ethics, and medicine, Mitchell and Riley engage real-life moral questions in a manner easily understood by laypersons and yet useful to clinicians, pastors, and students. This is a book to resource conversations in the home, lessons in the church, and understanding in the classroom. Mitchell and Riley invite readers to eavesdrop as they discuss the training of doctors, interpreting the Bible, and a range of pressing moral issues like abortion, assisted suicide, genetic engineering, and in vitro fertilization. While readers will find this volume to be biblically based, scientifically current, and accessible, they will also find it provides a healthy dose of empathy, engaging hearts as well as minds.

Daniel R. Heimbach
Series Editor

Acknowledgments

No book writes itself, and this one is no exception. We are both indebted to numerous individuals who have shaped our personal and professional lives and, therefore, this book. Ben's academic training in philosophy and medical ethics took place at the University of Tennessee at Knoxville (UTK). UTK had one of the earliest programs in clinical ethics of any university in the United States. It was begun in the early 1970s in Memphis under the tutelage of the late David Thomasma and migrated to Knoxville under the able direction of Glenn Graber, whose doctoral work had been done under William Frankena at Michigan. At UTK, Graber pioneered the case-based approach to clinical ethics that built upon the tradition of using cases for instruction in clinical medicine. Hence, nearly every chapter in this volume begins with a case for reflection.

Joy's informal training began at home, with parents Ely and Mary, who instilled in their children the truth that a good name is to be desired above riches. Her formal philosophy and medical ethics training began at the University of Louisville, with Richard L. Barber. Faculty members and attending physicians—too many to name individually—at the University of Kentucky College of Medicine and The Jewish Hospital of St. Louis, Washington University, modeled deep respect for and excellent care of patients. It was the mentors at Trinity International University who had the greatest impact, however: C. Ben Mitchell, Nigel M. de S. Cameron, Robert Orr, Edmund Pellegrino, John Kilner, and David Fletcher, among others. Dr. Cameron's use of the phrase, "making, taking, and faking life," made a lasting impression.

In addition to these formative influences, this volume has been improved by the series editor, Dan Heimbach, who offered many valuable questions and insights along the way. An unidentified reviewer deserves thanks also for the careful reading and thoughtful comments he or she made. Finally, it has been a genuine pleasure to work with Broadman and Holman's Chris Cowan. He has been very patient in the face of several delays. He has shepherded the process from the beginning with professionalism and grace. Thank you very much, Chris.

The volume is enhanced by the addition of visuals. For advice and assistance with those, we would like to thank Dr. Louis T. Riley, Dr. Christine Toevs, and Carol Harkness, a professional artist in the Nashville area. David W. Hobbs, project manager at LifeWay Christian Stores assisted with some of the graphics, as did his colleague, William Peter, a customer information analyst. L. Ian Riley of Ian Riley Photography provided graphics and photography. We would be remiss if we did not also thank Macy Alligood, an alumna of Union University, for her assistance in running down a boatload of footnotes.

As always, we must take blame for any errors in this volume. Additionally, we do not claim this to represent medical or legal advice. Despite any shortcomings, we trust it will be a helpful guide for thinking about the rocky crags we all must navigate in health care as we sail toward home.

Introduction

Phil and Sara have been happily married for two years. They are new Christians and have come to you for counseling because they were recently told they are infertile. Phil's sperm production is very low, and the doctor told them that if all else failed, they could use donor sperm and IVF to get pregnant.

They had several immediate questions: what in the world is donor sperm? What do the letters I-V-F stand for? Once those questions were answered, they would either have to find a suitable sperm donor themselves or purchase sperm from an anonymous donor at a sperm bank where they are told they could choose from a catalog of possible donors in hopes of having a child who might have some of the physical characteristics of the donor such as hair color, height, body type, and so on. This would give them better "quality control," as someone put it.

How would you counsel this couple? What emotional and spiritual issues are they likely to face? What ethical concerns do reproductive technologies, including sperm donation and in vitro fertilization, raise? Is the language of "quality control" problematic? Why or why not? Welcome to the real world of medical ethics.

Theology is as old as God. Although perhaps not quite as old, medicine has been around a long time. Historical evidence suggests that attempts to relieve human suffering through surgical interventions date back to around 9000 BC. And by 2000 BC the ancient law code of Hammurabi mandated that "if a surgeon performs a major operation on an 'awelum' (nobleman) with a lancet and caused the death of this man, they shall cut off his hands." So medical law and ethics have been around for a long time too.

"But this is the twenty-first century!" you exclaim. What does that have to do with making moral decisions about medical dilemmas in the real world? Great question. And that's the burden of this book: to help readers discover how biblical theology, Christian ethics, and contemporary science and medicine intersect in the real world where people are making life-changing decisions.

To help you make these discoveries, the two of us will let you in on our conversation. One of us is trained as a philosopher-theologian; the other is a physician. We both have degrees in medical ethics and long experience in the life of the church. Because we want our discussion to be helpful to pastors, family members, chaplains, physicians, students, and patients who are making decisions about their own medical treatment, we have tried to offer an accessible account of the medical, theological, and moral aspects of some of the ethical questions that arise in the care and treatment of real people. We've also tried to look into the future and think about where some of our medical technologies are taking us.

Theologian Nigel Cameron has helpfully categorized the issues in bioethics under the rubric of "taking life," "making life," and "remaking life." The order of these categories represents the order in which the ethical issues have arisen historically.

Taking Life

Euthanasia, assisted suicide, and abortion have long been within the purview of the ethics of medicine. Although Christians vary in their views of these issues, it is safe to say that Christians are life affirming. In fact, a vast majority of Christians would argue, for reasons to be seen in this book, that euthanasia and assisted suicide are inconsistent with the biblical witness on the sanctity of human life and the role of compassionate care in medicine. Likewise, most Christians believe that abortion on demand is wrong.

Typically, Christians are at the forefront of life-honoring alternatives. The early church, for instance, rescued children from infanticide by providing them with homes and building orphanages. Many contemporary Christians support pregnancy care centers that provide alternatives to abortion by offering pregnant mothers education, resources, and shelter as they await the delivery of their children. The hospice and palliative care movement was begun by a Christian nurse and physician, Dame Cicely Saunders, as a means of caring compassionately for those who are facing terminal illnesses.

Making Life

The ethical questions surrounding procreation fall under the category of "making life." Assisted reproductive technologies (ARTs) pose significant moral questions for Bible believers. Louise Brown, the world's first "test tube" baby was born in 1978. Since then in vitro fertilization (IVF) has been controversial. Additional reproductive arrangements, like surrogate motherhood, artificial insemination using donor sperm, and sperm or egg donation, introduce third parties or their gametes into the reproductive relationship. The Bible teaches that procreation is to take place within the context of a one-man, one-woman conjugal union. Bringing third parties into the procreative relationship is fraught with ethical, legal, social, and familial concerns. The relationship of Abraham, Sarah, and Hagar in the Old Testament illustrates the tensions that may be present in even low-tech reproductive relationships (Genesis 16). Adoption, however, has always been viewed as an ethical option for Christian couples facing infertility.

Remaking/Faking Life

Researchers are increasingly exploring new ways to mimic God's design. These new scientific technologies are usually regarded as laudable when used for healing purposes. Thus, the use of implantable computer chips to assist the blind to see is consistent with the goals of medicine. High-tech prostheses to replace limbs lost in accidents are likewise uncontroversial.

Using pharmaceuticals, like steroids, or genetic engineering to create higher than normal IQs or faster than normal athletes not only raises profound ethical questions about justice in academics or sports respectively, but also challenges our understanding of what it means to be human and who has the authority to alter our species.

Some suggest today that the use of life-prolonging technologies might enable us to live forever either in our physical bodies or uploaded into some vast neural network like the Internet. Again, while few question the use of technology for therapeutic purposes, many worry that enhancement technologies reveal a kind of hubris sometimes described as "playing God." After all, the Christian affirmation is that we are already immortal through the resurrection of Jesus Christ (1 Corinthians 15) and that our physical bodies will be transformed like his through our own resurrection and freed from the ravages of disease and death. The wise use of new technologies—medical or otherwise—must be part of Christian discipleship.

How to Use This Book

You will note that each chapter begins with a real case. The cases have come from news stories, casebooks, or our own experience. Although we do not attempt to deal with the cases directly, or even with every aspect of the cases, we do try to offer biblical, theological, and medical parameters to help you identify and think through some of the issues that arise in the cases. Each case ends with questions for reflection. We hope you will take the time individually, in small groups, or in classes to discuss the case study using those questions as a guide. After reading the chapter, it would be helpful to return to those questions to see if any answers have changed or if other questions arise.

We should be clear about our starting points. First, we are both committed to a Christian worldview. Among other things that means all truth genuinely deserving of the designation "truth" is God's truth. So we are not relativists. We believe that the true, the good, and the beautiful are found most clearly in the triune God of the Bible and seen most sublimely in the face of Jesus of Nazareth.

Second, we are both committed to historic orthodoxy. That is, we believe what the Christian church has affirmed down the ages in the Apostles' Creed:

> *I believe in God, the Father almighty,*
> *Creator of heaven and earth.*
> *I believe in Jesus Christ, his only Son, our Lord,*
> *who was conceived by the Holy Spirit,*
> *born of the virgin Mary,*
> *suffered under Pontius Pilate,*
> *was crucified, died, and was buried;*

he descended to the dead.
On the third day he rose again;
he ascended into heaven,
he is seated at the right hand of the Father,
and he will come to judge the living and the dead.
I believe in the Holy Spirit,
the holy catholic Church,
the communion of saints,
the forgiveness of sins,
the resurrection of the body,
and the life everlasting.
Amen.

Because we affirm that all truth is God's truth and because we believe this is God's world, we see science and faith, medicine and theology as friends, not enemies. That's not to say that all the tensions between them have been fully resolved, but it is to say that we think each of these realms of knowledge has some important information to offer us about the real world in which we live. And, just as importantly, we believe we neglect these sources of truth to our own peril and to the detriment of those we care about.

Finally, we believe that answers are available to some of the thorny questions that emerge at patients' bedsides. The resources God has supplied give us access to right, wrong, good, and bad ways of dealing with ethical questions in medicine and patient care. If we didn't believe that, we'd hardly have any reason to offer yet another book on bioethics.

Our prayer is that by the time you have read this book you will have a better idea how you would help Phil and Sara and the other people whose cases you will find in this volume.

Now, let's start at the beginning. . . .

Part I

Christian Bioethics

Chapter 1

Which Doctors? Whose Medicine?

Case: It's Over, Debbie

The call came in the middle of the night. As a gynecology resident rotating through a large, private hospital, I had come to detest telephone calls because invariably I would be up for several hours and would not feel good the next day. However, duty called, so I answered the phone. A nurse informed me that a patient was having difficulty getting rest. Could I please see her. She was on 3 North. That was the gynecologic-oncology unit, not my usual duty station. As I trudged along, bumping sleepily against walls and corners and not believing I was up again, I tried to imagine what I might find at the end of my walk. Maybe an elderly woman with an anxiety reaction or perhaps something particularly horrible.

I grabbed the chart from the nurses' station on my way to the patient's room, and the nurse gave me some hurried details: a twenty-year-old girl named Debbie was dying of ovarian cancer. She was having unrelenting vomiting apparently as the result of an alcohol drip administered for sedation. Very sad, I thought. As I approached the room, I could hear loud, labored breathing. I entered and saw an emaciated, dark-haired woman who appeared much older than twenty. She was receiving nasal oxygen, had an

IV, and was sitting in bed suffering from what was obviously severe air hunger. The chart noted her weight at eighty pounds. A second woman, also dark-haired but of middle age, stood at her right, holding her hand. Both looked up as I entered. The room seemed filled with the patient's desperate effort to survive. Her eyes were hollow, and she had suprasternal and intercostal retractions with her rapid inspirations. She had not eaten or slept in two days. She had not responded to chemotherapy and was being given supportive care only. It was a gallows scene, a cruel mockery of her youth and unfulfilled potential. Her only words to me were, "Let's get this over with."

I retreated with my thoughts to the nurses' station. The patient was tired and needed rest. I could not give her health, but I could give her rest. I asked the nurse to draw twenty mgs of morphine sulfate into a syringe. Enough, I thought, to do the job. I took the syringe into the room and told the two women I was going to give Debbie something that would let her rest and to say good-bye. Debbie looked at the syringe, then laid her head on the pillow with her eyes open, watching what was left of the world. I injected the morphine intravenously and watched to see if my calculations on its effects would be correct. Within seconds her breathing slowed to a normal rate, her eyes closed, and her features softened as she seemed restful at last. The older woman stroked the hair of the now-sleeping patient. I waited for the inevitable next effect of depressing the respiratory drive. With clocklike certainty, within four minutes the breathing rate slowed even more, then became irregular, then ceased. The dark-haired woman stood erect and seemed relieved.

It's over, Debbie.

—Name withheld by request[1]

Questions for Reflection

1. Why was the doctor called to see the patient? What did the
   doctor know about her?

---

[1] "A Piece of My Mind. It's Over, Debbie," *Journal of the American Medical Association* 259, no. 2 (January 8, 1988): 272.

2. What did Debbie mean when she said, "Let's get this over with"?

3. Comment on the physician's attitude toward this patient and her situation.

4. Describe the communication that occurred between doctor and patient, nurse and doctor, doctor and woman at the patient's bedside. What are the possible endings of this case?

5. What concerns might a Christian doctor or patient have in this situation that non-Christians may not have?

Discussion

C. Ben Mitchell (CBM): When I first encountered this story in graduate school, like most other readers I immediately thought this was a case of euthanasia. *Surely,* I thought, *the doctor must have given Debbie an overdose of morphine and killed her.* I now know that the case is open to multiple interpretations. The most important line is Debbie's, when she said: "Let's get this over with." Did she mean, "Please give me a life-ending drug"? Did she mean, "Please stop poking on me and give me some medication so I can get some sleep"? The case was meant to be ambiguous, of course. But in its context—in the late 1980s, in the world's most prestigious medical journal—the author was pushing the debate about assisted suicide and euthanasia. And he or she did. There was a huge response to this case in the letters to the editor pages of the journal and elsewhere. "It's Over, Debbie " continues to be used in medical schools and ethics programs across the country because it is so provocative.

The Hippocratic Oath
Debbie's case raises many interesting questions, including what the role of a physician is in treating his or her patients. Historically physicians took an oath that forbade them from intentionally ending

a patient's life through active means. It was called the Hippocratic Oath. It may surprise you to learn that most doctors do not take the oath today. But surely, you might say, a doctor's professional obligations would keep him from killing a patient. Actually, physicians' understanding of their professional obligations have changed dramatically over the last several decades.

As we begin to think about the ethics of medicine we must first understand who doctors are, who they *should* be, and what moral obligations doctors should feel with respect to their patients.

Dr. Riley, what can you tell us about the Hippocratic Oath and the tradition of which it is a part?

D. Joy Riley (DJR): Most people are familiar with the term "the Hippocratic Oath." They may have heard that doctors take the oath and presume physicians practice according to the ethical guidelines contained in it. In fact, although neither medicine nor medical ethics began with Hippocrates, much of Western medicine—at least for 2,500 years—does have its roots there. Unfortunately, though, most physicians know little about the oath.

Hippocrates of Cos (460–c. 370 BC), was a physician and the son of a physician. He is credited with a number of writings on medicine, though his followers were probably the authors of the Hippocratic Oath. The oath had three parts. First, the various deities were invoked. Second, the physician committed to care for his teacher and his teacher's family. Finally, he pledged to fulfill certain responsibilities toward his patients.

> I swear by Apollo the physician and Æsculapius, and Health, and All-heal, and all the gods and goddesses, that, according to my ability and judgment,
>
> I will keep this Oath and this stipulation—to reckon him who taught me this Art equally dear to me as my parents, to share my substance with him, and relieve his necessities if required; to look upon his offspring in the same footing as my own brothers, and to teach them this art, if they shall wish to learn it, without fee or stipulation; and that by precept, lecture, and every other mode of instruction,
>
> I will impart a knowledge of the Art to my own sons, and those of my teachers, and to disciples bound by a

stipulation and oath according to the law of medicine, but to none others.

I will follow that system of regimen which, according to my ability and judgement, I consider for the benefit of my patients, and abstain from whatever is deleterious and mischievous.

I will give no deadly medicine to any one if asked, nor suggest any such counsel; and in like manner I will not give to a woman a pessary to produce abortion. With purity and with holiness I will pass my life and practice my Art.

I will not cut persons labouring under the stone, but will leave this to be done by men who are practitioners of this work. Into whatever houses I enter, I will go into them for the benefit of the sick, and will abstain from every voluntary act of mischief and corruption; and, further, from the seduction of females or males, of freemen and slaves. Whatever, in connection with my professional service, or not in connection with it, I see or hear, in the life of men, which ought not to be spoken of abroad,

I will not divulge, as reckoning that all such should be kept secret. While I continue to keep this Oath unviolated, may it be granted to me to enjoy life and the practice of the art, respected by all men, in all times. But should I trespass and violate this Oath, may the reverse be my lot.

One way of thinking about the Hippocratic Oath is to see it as the covenant of an early physician's craft guild, medical society, or licensing authority. It was also the Better Business Bureau seal of approval, separating an ethical physician from the charlatans of the age. As such, it functioned to reform the practice of medicine.[2] Several features are worth noting. Hippocratic physicians refused to administer poisons for euthanasia or to perform abortions. They apparently were general practitioners since they referred patients to others for surgery. They foreswore sexual involvement with their patients and promised confidentiality. These were physicians a patient could trust.

---

[2] Allen Verhey, "The Doctor's Oath—and a Christian Swearing It," in *On Moral Medicine*, 3rd ed., ed. M. Therese Lysaught and Joseph J. Kotva Jr., with Stephen E. Lammers and Allen Verhey (Grand Rapids, MI: Eerdmans, 2012), 226.

CBM: So a physician in the Hippocratic tradition entered a covenant with the gods, his teachers, and his patients. Yet the original oath was pagan? Did Christians and Jews ever embrace the oath?

DJR: Yes, the original Hippocratic Oath called on the deities of the Greek world. In addition, Ludwig Edelstein, the distinguished medical historian, suggests that physicians who took the oath were also followers of the philosopher, mathematician, and mystic Pythagoras.[3] They were mostly polytheists.

Because it was generally recognized that the Hippocratic Oath required appropriate commitments by the doctors who took it, a Christianized form of the oath was circulated by the tenth century AD. In it the "Greek divinities are replaced by 'God the Father of our Lord Jesus Christ,' the prohibition of abortion is strengthened, and the stricture against 'cutting for the stone' is dropped."[4]

About the same time that the Lateran Council II (1139) allowed monks to practice medicine within certain limits,[5] one of the great Jewish physicians was born. Maimonides, who lived 1135–1204, was a philosopher as well as a physician and Talmudist. He summarized the Hippocratic dictum as "be of benefit and do no harm." Maimonides reflected on the behavior of physicians and concluded, "There is a general rule, and I have seen great physicians acting on it, that the physician should not treat the disease but the patient who is suffering from it."[6]

Whatever the preamble of the oath(s) taken, physicians of various faiths throughout the centuries have adopted many of the Hippocratic Oath's valued stances. I am sure you understand why Christians would be interested in medicine and caring for the sick.

CBM: I do indeed. Historically, the people of God have been leaders in medicine and the building of hospitals because they believe all truth is God's truth and that medicine offers great good. For instance, the second-century BC apocryphal book *Ecclesiasticus* teaches that medicine owes its origins to God: "Honor the

---

[3] Albert R. Jonsen, *A Short History of Medical Ethics* (New York: Oxford University Press, 2000), 4.

[4] Ibid., 17.

[5] Ibid.

[6] Ibid., 22.

physician . . . from God the physician gets wisdom. . . . God brings forth medicines from the earth and let a prudent man not ignore them" (39:1). Of course, Luke, author of Acts and the gospel that bears his name, was a physician. The early church not only endorsed medicine but championed care for the sick because Jesus of Nazareth healed the sick during his ministry on earth (see Matt 9; 10:8; 25:34–46).

Admittedly, the Greeks and Romans made great contributions to early medicine, but as Albert Jonsen, University of Washington historian of medicine, maintains: "The second great sweep of medical history begins at the end of the fourth century, with the founding of the first Christian hospital at Caesarea in Cappadocia, and concludes at the end of the fourteenth century, with medicine well ensconced in the universities and in the public life of the emerging nations of Europe."[7] This extraordinary, formative period in medicine was characterized by intimate involvement by the church. Jonsen argues:

> During these centuries, the Christian faith . . . permeated all aspects of life in the West. The very conception of medicine, as well as its practice, was deeply touched by the doctrine and discipline of the Church. This theological and ecclesiastical influence shaped the ethics of medicine, but it even indirectly affected its science since, as its missionaries evangelized the peoples of Western and Northern Europe, the Church found itself in a constant battle against the use of magic and superstition in the work of healing. It championed rational medicine, along with prayer, to counter superstition.[8]

As a means of caring for those who were ill, Saint Basil of Caesarea founded the first hospital (c. 369). Christian hospitals grew apace, spreading throughout both the East and the West. By the mid-1500s there were 37,000 Benedictine monasteries alone that cared for the sick.

---

[7] Ibid., 13.
[8] Ibid.

Furthermore, as Charles Rosenberg shows in his volume, *The Care of Strangers: The Rise of America's Hospital System*,[9] the modern hospital owes its origins to Judeo-Christian compassion. The vast expansion of faith-based hospitals is seen in the legacy of their names: Saint Vincent's, Saint Luke's, Mount Sinai, Presbyterian, Mercy, and Beth Israel. These were all charitable hospitals, some of which began as foundling hospitals to care for abandoned children.

Similarly, in Europe, great hospitals were built through the influence of the church. Indeed, an ancient French term for hospital is *hôtel-Dieu* ("hostel of God"). In 1863, the *Société Genevoise d'Utilité Publique* called on Swiss Christian businessman Jean Henri Dunant to form a relief organization for caring for wartime wounded. Thus, one year later the Geneva Convention made the Red Cross a universal sign of medical care. In Britain, Dame Cicely Saunders founded the hospice movement by establishing Saint Christopher's Hospice in the south of London in 1967.

Things have certainly changed. Most religious hospitals today are religious in name only. What about the use of the Hippocratic Oath? Is it still in use? Did you learn about the oath in your own medical training?

DJR: Somewhat surprisingly, most medical schools do not use the Hippocratic Oath today. Those who do offer some kind of "updated" version of it. My own experience in medical school is probably fairly typical. After four years of training (and an extra year of a student pathology fellowship for good measure), I graduated from medical school. Our institution's version of the oath was printed on the back of our graduation program, and we were asked to stand and read the oath in unison. Few if any of us had seen it in advance. There had been no examination or discussion of the oath beforehand.

I may have been a bit more familiar with it than some of my peers since before medical school I had taken a number of undergraduate philosophy courses, including a medical ethics class. I also

---

[9] In 1800, with a population of only 5.3 million, most Americans would only have heard of a hospital. Philadelphia's Pennsylvania Hospital was founded in 1751, New York Hospital in 1771, and Boston General did not open until 1821. But by just after the mid-century mark, hospitals were being established in large numbers, and most of them were religious. Charles E. Rosenberg, *The Care of Strangers: The Rise of America's Hospital System* (New York: Basic, 1987), esp. chap. 4.

took the one elective course in medical ethics our medical school offered. During medical school we were taught by some excellent, caring, competent, and ethical physicians. But they offered little didactic teaching on the kinds of ethical principles contained in the oath of Hippocrates.

Our school was not unusual. A survey of US medical schools in the mid-1990s showed only one school used the original oath. The data from that survey are included in table 1.

Table 1
Survey of 157 medical schools in the mid-1990s: 1 school used the original Oath 68 schools used some version of the Oath 8% prohibited abortion 14% prohibited euthanasia and assisted suicide 43% included some notion of MD accountability 3% forbade sexual contact with patients
Orr, R. D., N. Pang, E. D. Pellegrino, and M. Siegler. 1997. "Use of the Hippocratic Oath: A Review of Twentieth-Century Practice and a Content Analysis of Oaths Administered in Medical Schools in the U.S. and Canada in 1993." The Journal of Clinical Ethics 8 (Winter): 377-388.

What happened? Medical ethics, traditionally the arena of physicians, was opened up to other voices in the twentieth century. In 1968, Senator Walter Mondale called a congressional hearing to discuss "the social implications of advances in medicine and the biosciences." This was not welcomed by the scientific and medical communities. They saw it as an intrusion. Dr. Owen Wangansteen, professor at the University of Minnesota, said, "If you are thinking of theologians, lawyers, philosophers and others to give some direction, . . . I cannot see how they could help. . . . The fellow who holds the apple can peel it best."[10]

That attitude, however, did not prevent the birth of bioethics as we know it. Interestingly, when people began to look for experts who understood something about the moral values involved in life-and-death decision making, they identified several theological voices.

Birth of Bioethics

CBM: That's right. Among the first was Paul Ramsey. Ramsey was the Harrington Spear Pain Professor of Religion at Princeton

---

[10] Cited in Paul Ramsey, *The Patient as Person: Exploration in Medical Ethics*, 2nd ed. (New Haven, CT: Yale University Press, 2002), xvii.

University and the author of *The Patient as Person*, published in 1970. This work, presented the previous year as the Lyman Beecher Lectures at Yale, raises many important questions about informed consent, research involving children, changing the definition of death, and organ transplantation, among other problems. In his preface to that book, Ramsey states, "At this point physicians must in greater measure become moral philosophers, asking themselves some quite profound questions about the nature of proper moral reasoning, and how moral dilemmas are rightly to be resolved. If they do not, the existing medical ethics will be eroded more and more by what it is alleged *must* be done and technically *can* be done."[11]

Another early leader was Richard A. McCormick, who wrote about theology and bioethics from his Catholic view and experience. Like the followers of Hippocrates, McCormick saw theological language as a way of thinking about the ethics of medicine and used Christian categories in his discussion of the morality of medicine "since goodness-badness is basically vertical and has its aortal lifeline to the God-relationship."[12]

As a Catholic thinker McCormick rejected what he saw as two extremes. He denied that "faith gives us concrete answers to the problems of *essential* ethics," or norms that apply to all persons. He also refuted the position that "faith has no influence whatsoever on bioethics."[13] He argued for reason informed by faith.

McCormick believed our culture was becoming increasingly inhospitable to the vulnerable, especially the "defective" or "maladapted." He argued that faith could protect from such an attitude because faith "does sensitize us to the meaning of persons, to their inherent dignity regardless of functionability."[14] Christian faith engenders certain dispositions toward others, particularly that of charity. Finally, he thought life was "a basic but not absolute good."[15] As he put it: "Excessive concern for the temporal is at some point neglect of the eternal. An obligation to use all means to preserve life would be a devaluation of human life, since it would

---

[11] Ibid., xlviii.

[12] Richard A. McCormick, "Theology and Bioethics," *Hastings Center Report* 19, no. 3 (May/June 1989): 5–10. Reprinted in Stephen E. Lammers and Allen Verhey, eds., *On Moral Medicine*, 2nd ed. (Grand Rapids, MI: Eerdmans, 1998), 65.

[13] Ibid., 67.

[14] Ibid., 68.

[15] Ibid., 70.

remove life from the context or story that is the source of its ultimate value."[16]

The third theologian to make major contributions to the field of bioethics was Joseph Fletcher, professor of moral theology at Episcopal Theological School (Cambridge, Massachusetts). His background was in social justice. He is perhaps best known for his book *Situation Ethics*. After he turned his focus to medical ethics, he became a professor of medical ethics at the University of Virginia.[17]

DJR: Frankly, I think one of the reasons medical schools today do not regard the oath as authoritative could be due to the influence of Joseph Fletcher and others like him. As early as 1949, in the Lowell Lectures at Harvard, Fletcher said, "[W]e shall attempt, as reasonably as may be, to plead the ethical case for our human rights (certain conditions being satisfied) to use contraceptives, to seek insemination anonymously from a donor, to be sterilized, and to receive a merciful death from a medically competent euthanasiast."[18]

Albert R. Jonsen called this "revolutionary," and this description was accurate. No longer was it the physician or the church who "held authority over the body and mind of the patient." It was the patient's right and his alone to make his own medical decision.[19] The idea of patients' rights gathered steam as the twentieth century progressed. Joseph Fletcher personified this development, but he was not alone. The result has been a shift in the character of medicine away from professionalism toward a market-based medicine, complete with customers who are supposedly "always right." What was perceived as paternalism has now given way to consumerism.

CBM: Most of us have grown up in the era of "consumer medicine." If doctors are not to be viewed as members of the "service industry," how should we understand their role?

---

[16] Ibid.

[17] Jonsen, *A Short History of Medical Ethics*, 94–95.

[18] Joseph Fletcher, *Morals and Medicine* (Boston: Beacon, 1954), 25, cited in Jonsen, *A Short History of Medical Ethics*, 94.

[19] Jonsen, *A Short History of Medical Ethics*, 94.

DJR: Physicians have been variously considered as parent figures, fighters (think *M*A*S*H**), and, increasingly, as technicians. William F. May describes—and rejects—these three metaphors in his important book, *The Physician's Covenant.* Paternalism in medicine is an anemic substitute for something greater because, according to May, that model "keenly experiences the absence of divine providence and substitutes a providence of its own."[20] Similarly, if physicians are seen primarily as fighters, suffering and the fear of death contend to be the *summum malum* (the supreme evil). He correctly argues, I think, that viewing physicians primarily as technicians does not end well either: "The cumulative impact of the training filters out the personal, not merely the patient as person but the physician as person."[21] May concludes, then, that the best metaphors for understanding the physician's role in the physician-patient relationship are those of covenant and teacher. He states, "A covenantal ethic positions human givers in the context of a primordial act of receiving a gift not wholly deserved, which they can only assume gratefully."[22] This provides a richer, and, I believe, a more appropriate view of the physician's role than any of the other metaphors.

CBM: This brings us back to the case of Debbie. What is your interpretation of the physician's behavior in "It's Over, Debbie"?

DJR: I find the physician's behavior problematic in several ways. (To simplify the discussion with respect to pronouns, I will refer to the physician as "he.") The physician is paternalistic in that he seems to think he knows what Debbie wants on the basis of a single uttered sentence. There is no discussion of her statement, "Let's get this over with," much less any meaningful consent from the patient. In this case the physician is a warrior, and wakefulness seems to be the enemy. It appears that sleep in some form—for the patient, the patient's mother(?), and the physician—is the victory to be obtained. The physician authoritatively takes charge. The nurse is only there to fill the syringe. As the technician the physician administers the drug. He administers a large dose of

---

[20] William F. May, *The Physician's Covenant: Images of the Healer in Medical Ethics,* 2nd ed. (Louisville: WJK, 2000), 54.
[21] Ibid., 103.
[22] Ibid., 114.

morphine, which like clockwork produces a kind of sleep followed by respiratory depression and, presumably, death—for a woman the physician had met for the first time only moments before. The "problem" has been conquered efficiently, even if it meant ending the patient's life.

CBM: Obviously, if one finds *parent, warrior,* and *technician* unacceptable metaphors for *physician,* then another metaphor is necessary. How would you suggest we think about the role of physicians?

DJR: The late physicians Edmund Pellegrino and David Thomasma stressed the need for virtuous physicians. Because doctors have the power to diagnose and treat and because patients are vulnerable and experiencing unease, trust is a necessary foundation for their relationship. A patient needs to be able to trust that the physician will use his/her knowledge, training, and skill to do what will benefit, not exploit, the patient. And physicians need to be worthy of that trust.

> In an ethic of trust, the physician is impelled to develop a relationship with the patient from the very outset that includes becoming familiar with who and what the patient is and how she wants to meet the serious challenges of illness, disability, and death. It is essential that the physician help the patient to anticipate certain critical decisions. . . . The physician must prepare the patient for these eventualities before they become urgent or the patient loses competence. Patients should be able to rely on the physician for the proper timing, sensitivity, and degree of detail appropriate in each case. These cannot be written into a contract.[23]

Trust, according to Pellegrino and Thomasma, goes beyond duty or rule-based ethics, although it is "consistent with the contemporary context of autonomy, participatory democracy, and the moral pluralism of the interacting parties in professional relationships."[24]

---

[23] Edmund D. Pellegrino and David C. Thomasma, *The Virtues in Medical Practice* (New York: Oxford University Press, 1993), 76. See also their volume, *The Christian Virtues in Medical Practice* (Washington, DC: Georgetown University Press, 1996).
[24] Ibid., 77.

It is based in virtue, which begets character. It begins in a relationship and is built over time, "earned and merited by performance and fidelity to its implications."[25]

For the physician several virtues are essential. The first is compassion, a "suffering with" the patient. Prudence guides doctors in proper action, toward the proper end of medicine. That proper end is twofold. "The ultimate end is the health of individuals and society, while the more proximate end is a right and good healing action for a specific patient."[26] Justice includes not simply giving one his/her due but doing so in a spirit of friendship or charity. Another virtue to be cultivated by physicians is fortitude, or "sustained courage."[27] Medical temperance is described by "constant vigilance about protecting persons from undertreatment, abandonment, and inappropriate overtreatment,"[28] a virtue sorely needed in this day. Pellegrino and Thomasma round out their discussion of the virtues with integrity and self-effacement. Doctors should work hard to be trust-*worthy* and humble.

CBM: That is a helpful summary. Much more has been written about the virtuous physician, and the idea is certainly worthy of more in-depth study. You and I both knew Dr. Pellegrino and heard him speak multiple times over the years. He was an excellent and prolific writer and a virtuous clinician. Today's physicians in training may not be able to know him personally, but the paper trail he left could never be mistaken for mere breadcrumbs.

Conclusion

We are a long way from Hippocratic medicine. Medical ethics has undergone a sea change. We need to regain the higher moral ground to achieve the proper ends of medicine. That begins with a physician-patient relationship built on trust. This requires both virtuous physicians and virtuous patients. Physician education should include not only superb scientific training but also excellent ethical instruction. Most importantly, those who care for vulnerable patients should be men and women of good character.

---

[25] Ibid.
[26] Ibid., 86.
[27] Ibid., 109.
[28] Ibid., 124–25.

Remembering where moral medicine has come from may be a useful way of guiding the future.

The Hippocratic Oath, though little used today, has impacted the practice of medicine over centuries and continents. How does that happen? How do we proceed from an ancient text to contemporary decisions? The next chapter offers a way forward.

Additional Resources

Cameron, Nigel M. de S. *The New Medicine: Life and Death After Hippocrates*. Chicago: Bioethics, 2001.

Groopman, Jerome. *How Doctors Think*. New York: Mariner, 2008.

Lysaught, M. Therese, and Joseph J. Kotva Jr., with Stephen E. Lammers and Allen Verhey, eds. *On Moral Medicine: Theological Perspectives in Medical Ethics*, 3rd ed. Grand Rapids, MI: Eerdmans, 2012.

Overby, Philip. "The Moral Education of Doctors." *The New Atlantis*, Fall 2005. Accessed March 8, 2011, http://www.thenewatlantis.com/publications/the-moral-education-of-doctors.

Chapter 2

From Ancient Book to the
Twenty-First Century

Case: Stem Cell Discovery Could Put
Cloning on the Fast Track[1]

The accepted understanding for decades has been that a female is born with all the eggs she will ever have. That understanding was suddenly called into question when the finding of human ovarian stem cells was announced in 2012. Based on studies of mouse ovaries, in which were found stem cells that could produce mouse eggs, human ovaries were examined to see if similar stem cells could be found there. Where does one obtain fresh young human ovaries? In this case six Japanese women, who were undergoing sex reassignment procedures, donated their ovaries for the research.

Jonathan Tilly and colleagues at Massachusetts General Hospital found that the ovary's oogonial stem cells (OSCs) generated normal-appearing immature oocytes (eggs) in laboratory culture. Evelyn Telfer, a reproductive biologist at the University

---

[1] Rebecca Taylor, "Stem Cell Discovery Could Put Cloning on the Fast Track," March 5, 2012, accessed December 4, 2013, http://www.lifenews.com/2012/03/05/stem-cell -discovery-could-put-cloning-on-the-fast-track.

25

of Edinburgh, "noted that there's still no evidence that the OSCs form new eggs naturally in the body. However, if they could be coaxed in a dish to make eggs that could successfully be used for *in vitro* fertilization (IVF), it would change the face of assisted reproduction."[2]

Rebecca Taylor, at LifeNews.com, was unsettled by the enthusiasm for this finding:

> But I want to talk about a few realities. First, the reality of using eggs grown in the lab to make embryos in a lab. Starting out life in a dish with naturally made eggs is already a dangerous prospect. Children conceived with IVF are 9 times more likely to have the genetic disorder Beckwith-Wiedemann's Syndrome. Some recent studies are suggesting that people conceived with IVF have different patterns of gene expression than those conceived naturally and so are at greater risk for major disease like obesity and diabetes later in life. And it is estimated that 90% of IVF embryos have chromosomal abnormalities.
>
> How much greater will the genetic risks be with eggs grown artificially? What does that mean for the offspring? Does anyone care? I have not seen a single commentary questioning the safety for the children that would be produced. Are we all too busy simply wondering if it can be done to wonder if it should be done?[3]

Could the discovery of egg stem cells reignite the interest in embryonic stem cells from cloned embryos, known as "therapeutic cloning" or somatic cell nuclear transfer (SCNT)? The interest, so prevalent after Dolly the cloned sheep made her debut, has waned somewhat in the public consciousness due to two primary factors, according to Taylor: (1) The sheer number of eggs needed for cloning was daunting: not enough women volunteered their eggs for this research. (2) Induced pluripotent stem cells (iPS cells)—stem cells produced without either eggs or cloning—had many of the

---

[2] Kendall Powell, "Egg-Making Stem Cells Found in Adult Ovaries," *Nature News* 27 (February 2012), accessed October 30 2013, http://www.nature.com/news/egg-making-stem-cells-found-in-adult-ovaries-1.10121.

[3] Taylor, "Stem Cell Discovery Could Put Cloning on the Fast Track."

characteristics of embryonic stem cells but without the hassle. She concludes:

> And yet there are those that want to continue with cloning research. The promise of a greater supply of eggs using these stem cells found in ovaries has people talking about therapeutic cloning again. And as many experts believe, therapeutic cloning, cloning embryos for research, is only a stop on the road to reproductive cloning, cloning embryos to produce children. Gregory Pence, philosophy professor at the University of Alabama at Birmingham and cloning advocate, rightly observed in his book, *Cloning After Dolly: Who's Still Afraid?*, "Scientists are naive to think they can ban reproductive cloning and go ahead studying embryonic [therapeutic] cloning."
>
> So this discovery has much greater ramifications than simply slowing a woman's biological clock. If successful, this technique may put the push for cloning back on the fast track.[4]

Questions for Reflection

1. How does the Bible apply to making health care and bioresearch decisions in the contemporary world? How should Christians use the Bible, and to what degree, when dealing with questions arising in bioethics?

2. What are stem cells, and where do they come from?

3. Who decides what risks are appropriate for embryos/children?

4. When should new technologies be embraced? What assurances of safety are needed before society can welcome a novel technology?

---

[4] Ibid.

5. Do you think cloning is a realistic goal? Do you think the author's fears are well founded?

6. What biblical norms or principles, if any, apply to medical technologies that did not exist when the Bible was written?

✛

Discussion

D. Joy Riley (DJR): We are living in an increasingly fast-paced and highly technological world, especially in biomedicine and biotechnology. The twenty-first century is truly upon us with all its wonderful possibilities and its pressing moral dilemmas. Stem cells, cloning, and human egg donation are not mentioned in the Bible. Nor is there any reference in the Bible to more common entities like ventilator support, organ donation, or coronary artery bypass grafts. How do we move from the ancient biblical text to twenty-first-century questions? After all, the Bible is neither a science textbook nor a manual of medicine. How do we employ the Scriptures of the Old and New Testaments to make decisions about health care or biotechnology?

C. Ben Mitchell (CBM): The short answer is that, as the apostle Peter told the faithful Christians in Asia minor, "[God's] divine power has given us everything required for life and godliness through the knowledge of Him who called us by His own glory and goodness" (2 Pet 1:3). In other words, God has not left his people without guidance in every area of life. Although the Bible is not a science textbook, its message speaks to the deep underlying values that can guide decisions about scientific matters. Although the Bible is not a manual of medicine, its truths may be applied to medical decision making.

DJR: You have written about how Christians understand the Bible in reference to ethics. Could you explain this?

CBM: Christians have understood the role of the Bible in ethics in a number of ways. Here are a few of the most popular views:

The Bible as Law Code

Some Christians understand the Bible to be a book of eternal laws. They argue that if people want to know what they should do, they should consult the commandments and ordinances of the Old and New Testaments. Interestingly, this often turns out to be a popular Christian version of the way the Jewish rabbis understood the Old Testament. The ancient rabbis taught that the Torah (the first five books of the Old Testament) could be summarized in 613 commandments or *mitzvot*. Living ethically meant keeping all 613 laws. Some Christians treat the Ten Commandments, the teachings of Jesus, the prescriptions of Paul, or all three, the same way the rabbis treated the *mitzvot*. Find a rule and follow it.

DJR: This seems a fairly straightforward approach: divine command theory, is it not?

CBM: Well, I might call it a naïve divine command theory of ethics. The problem with this way of applying Scripture is that it is too simplistic. The Bible is much more than a book of rules. The sixty-six books of the Old and New Testaments do, indeed, include commandments and precepts. They also include historical, wisdom, and prophetic literature. There are songs, poems, and letters. If Christians are to take seriously the entire body of God's revelation in the Bible, they must take seriously the variety of ways in which God has revealed his will.

The Bible as Universal Principles

Another way Christians approach the biblical material is to see it as a source of principles to be discerned for ethical decision making. This view understands that the Old and New Testaments are historically situated and cannot always translate easily into a contemporary context. So, rather than look for specific commandments, these Christians attempt to discern the underlying principles they believe inform those commandments.

For instance, the Old Testament tells God's people not to round off the hair on their temples (Lev 19:27) or mix different types of fabric (Lev 19:19). These texts are part of the "Holiness Code" (Leviticus 17–26), a section of Leviticus that emphasizes both the holiness of God and the way his people are to be holy and set apart from the pagan nations around them. Christians do not understand these commands to be applied literally today, but they do believe the underlying principle applies, namely, that God's people are to be holy and set apart from the pagan culture around them. Christians are to be identifiable as God's own people in their behavior and practices.

Seeing the Bible as a book of universal principles is also fraught with difficulties. First, as with the Bible as Law Code view, this perspective does not take into account the rich diversity of biblical teaching about ethics. In some cases in the Bible, we are given persons to imitate rather than principles to apply. The Beatitudes Jesus taught in the Sermon on the Mount (Matt 5:3–10), for instance, are not principles to be followed but virtues to be lived and cultivated. Second, because identification of the principles depends on our discernment, we must be careful that we have perceived and applied them correctly. This is not always easily done.

The Bible as Community Narrative

Some scholars emphasize the Bible as a grand narrative, a sacred story of God's redemptive acts among his people. Living faithfully, they argue, means situating oneself in the story and living accordingly. The people of God—the church—are to see themselves as participants in the narrative. This view helpfully points out that the thirty-nine books of the Old Testament and twenty-seven books of the New Testament, despite their genres, contexts, and time periods, form a cohesive drama with leading characters, heroes and villains, plots and twists, morals and lessons, and a climactic ending. In fact, one of the evidences of divine authorship of the Bible is the way it holds together from Genesis to Revelation.

But the Bible is not only narrative. Some of the Bible is didactic, some is poetic, and some is epistolary. Scripture contains timeless rules. The problem with understanding the Bible as merely a story is that one may be tempted to neglect those timeless rules and enduring principles.

DJR: So if none of these views does justice to the biblical text, how should we understand the role of the Bible in Christian decision-making?

The Bible as Canonical Revelation of Divine Commands and Christian Virtues

CBM: The Bible should be understood, I would argue, as a canonical revelation of God's commands and Christian virtues. First, it is canonical. That is to say, the Bible is the book of the church. The books included in the canon (meaning "rule" or "measuring stick") were recognized as divinely inspired and authoritative. Those books are the church's only rule of faith and practice.

Second, they are revelation. God has made himself and his will known in the Scriptures of the Old and New Testaments. As Saint Paul said to young pastor Timothy, "All Scripture is inspired by God and is profitable for teaching, for rebuking, for correcting, for training in righteousness, so that the man of God may be complete, equipped for every good work" (2 Tim 3:16–17). The confession of the church has been that God's revelation is a sufficient guide for knowing his will. Furthermore, the books of the Bible reflect various types of literature, including history, poetry, wisdom, prophecy, apocalyptic, and letters. Accurate interpretation and proper application require that readers attend to the type of literature, the historical context, and the aim of each of those texts.

Third, God's moral instruction comes to us in the form of commands and principles and is also revealed in Christian virtues and examples. No one can (or should) deny that the Bible contains rules or commands. The Ten Commandments, for instance, stand as a lasting testimony to God's will for human flourishing. Likewise, enduring principles can be derived from the biblical witness. Even though the Bible does not include a direct commandment forbidding the use of human beings as experimental guinea pigs against their wills, the principle of human dignity, grounded in the image of God, applies. Because they are made in the image of God, research should not be done on human subjects without their consent. (Note: And because people are made in God's image, some research should not be conducted regardless of consent because it would violate human personhood.)

Furthermore, not only does the Bible contain eternal commandments and universal principles, but it also contains biographies of virtuous individuals, most notably Jesus of Nazareth, and descriptions of virtues to be cultivated by his followers. God has revealed himself in Jesus Christ, the Word made flesh (John 1). In the person of Christ, we see the epitome of what a virtuous human being is. As both fully divine and fully human, Jesus is our exemplar. Likewise, Jesus' teaching includes commands, principles, and virtues. As already mentioned, the Sermon on the Mount (Matthew 5–7) begins with a list of Beatitudes or descriptions of the happily virtuous Christian. Poverty of spirit, mournfulness, meekness, hungering for righteousness, and so on (Matt 5:3–12) are not rules to be followed but virtues to be inhabited. Much of the remainder of the sermon includes commands not to be angry, lust, divorce, take oaths, or retaliate. Positively, Jesus commands his disciples to love their enemies, give to those in need, pray single-heartedly, fast, and store up treasures in heaven rather than on earth. In addition to Jesus' example and instruction, the apostle Paul provides several lists of virtues that are to mark the Christian. Faith, hope, and love (1 Cor 13:13) combine to make up the so-called theological virtues. Among other virtues are the fruit of the Spirit, those virtues the Holy Spirit cultivates in the believer's life: "But the fruit of the Spirit is love, joy, peace, patience, kindness, goodness, faithfulness, gentleness, self-control. Against such things there is no law. Now those who belong to Christ Jesus have crucified the flesh with its passions and desires" (Gal 5:22–24). They describe the character of the faithful Christian and are to be operative in our decision making. And in more than one place Paul enjoins other Christians to "imitate me" (1 Cor 4:16; 11:1) even as he is an imitator of God in Christ (1 Cor 11:1; Eph 5:1).

DJR: That is a helpful explication of how you see Scripture rightly used in its application to ethics. Should we be aware of other nuances?

CBM: In his helpful volume, *Exploring Christian Ethics: Biblical Foundations for Morality*, Kyle Fedler offers some helpful guidelines about how to use Scripture. First, he says, realize that no single method for using Scripture is adequate. "The very diversity of the Bible itself warns us against a simplistic use."[5] Interpret stories as story, history as history, epistles as epistles, and poetry as poetry.

[5] Kyle D. Fedler, *Exploring Christian Ethics: Biblical Foundations for Morality* (Louisville: WJK, 2006), 61.

Second, whenever possible Scripture should be read in its historical and cultural context.[6] The first question we should ask of a given text is, "What did the original readers and hearers understand the text to mean?" This means we will need to situate ourselves as much as possible in the historical-cultural context of those original hearers. Knowing certain features of the history, geography, and climate of the ancient Near East may be helpful in understanding some texts. The biblical languages (Hebrew in the Old Testament and Greek and Aramaic in the New Testament) will often yield important insights about the way words were used. Archaeological discoveries may open up the meaning of certain passages of the Bible.

Third, Fedler reminds us that not all Scripture carries the same normative weight.[7] For instance, some commands under the old covenant must be reinterpreted in light of the new covenant. The Old Testament prescriptions about animal sacrifice have all found their fulfillment in the sacrifice of Jesus, the Lamb of God. Although principles of the Holiness Code in Leviticus may be morally obligatory today, the letter of the law is not. In other words, we cannot proof text to find answers to our moral questions. We cannot lift a Bible verse out of its literary, historical, and cultural context and expect to find help in decision making.

Finally, although Scripture is primary, normative, and authoritative, it is not our only source of guidance and wisdom.[8] Tradition, the way the church has dealt with similar cases in the past, may illuminate our understanding of the present. Experience—especially in our case, scientific knowledge—will obviously be important in understanding the truth of the matter. And, while we must not rely on human wisdom alone, the faculty of reason often helps provide clarity about the moral questions of a case and can help us determine an appropriate course of action.

So the Bible has much to offer believers as they seek to obey the Lord in every area of life, but it's not always as easy as matching one Bible verse with a problem. As you have already pointed out, no biblical texts speak directly to questions about human cloning or embryonic stem cell research or artificial intelligence. Careful attention must be paid, then, to discern the commands, principles,

---

[6] Ibid.
[7] Ibid., 61–62.
[8] Ibid., 62.

and virtues that apply in a particular context. We will see this in practice as we consider various examples throughout this book.

Interestingly, not only must we pay careful attention to the Bible as we make decisions about health care, but we must also pay careful attention to science and medicine. This is why we began in chapter 1 with a discussion of the nature and history of medicine. Medicine has many goals and aims, but its primary aim is to serve the patient's good.

Can you describe the sources or kinds of information that must be understood and interpreted from a medical point of view?

DJR: Whatever its deficiencies, modern medical science seems nearly miraculous in its powers to heal. Contemporary Westerners have difficulty imagining what life, sickness, and death were like before the dawn of scientific medicine. Much has been learned since the days of Hippocrates, and we are the beneficiaries of millennia of scientific discoveries. For instance, Galen, who lived from AD 129 to 216 and served as doctor to Marcus Aurelius, was trained in philosophy and Greek literature and brought Plato's systems of the body and Aristotle's logic to the study of medicine. He was known for his diagnostic acumen, using "palpation, pulse-taking, and occasionally the inspection of urine"[9] in his work. Despite Galen's advances, however, physicians were confronted with diseases that sometimes wiped out wide swaths of the population: malaria, tuberculosis, syphilis, influenza, the "black death," smallpox, cholera, and a host of others. Yet, "for centuries medicine was impotent and hence unproblematic. From the Greeks to the First World War, its job was simple: to struggle with lethal diseases and gross disabilities, to ensure live births, and to manage pain. It performed these uncontroversial tasks mostly with meagre success."[10]

Medieval physicians typically believed four elemental bodies— earth, fire, water, and air—gave rise to four humors in the body. In sickness these humors were out of balance, and the kind of illness, its treatment, as well as whether the patient would recover, were in some way dependent on the position of the moon and stars.[11]

---

[9] Roy Porter, ed., *The Cambridge Illustrated History of Medicine* (Cambridge, UK: Cambridge University Press, 1996; paperback edition, 2001), 62.
[10] Ibid.
[11] Walter Clyde Curry, *Chaucer and the Mediaeval Sciences* (New York: Oxford University Press, 1926), 10–11.

CBM: You are trained as an allopathic physician. There are also osteopaths, homeopaths, and others. Who is who?

DJR: Christian Friedrich Samuel Hahnemann, a physician in Germany in the late 1700s, founded homeopathy. His theory was that if a certain medication given to a healthy person produces mild symptoms like those present in more florid form in a disease, then that medication can be used to treat the disease. Homeopathic remedies, typically herbal, were used in infinitesimal doses.[12] Mary Baker Eddy, the American founder of the Christian Science movement, published her *Science and Health* in 1875. She dismissed matter as an illusion; therefore, afflictions of pain or sickness were illusory and required healing of the mind.[13]

Other disciplines have arisen as well. Chiropractic medicine endorses the manipulation of the spine to address disease. Osteopathy, originally treating disorders with muscle and bone manipulation, often now includes aspects of conventional or, what is also known as allopathic medicine, the discipline most recognizable as "medicine" in the Western world today. Nursing plays a supportive and indispensable role in allopathic medicine, and a number of ancillary services to modern-day medicine have practitioners who have been trained with a primarily allopathic model.

Allopathic medical schools typically have a four-year curriculum; this is followed by residency training of another three to seven years, depending on the specialty discipline. The first year of a residency is called an internship. After the residency one can be further trained in a fellowship. Each field of medicine—surgery, OB/GYN, internal medicine, pediatrics, to name a few—has its own requirements for training time and qualifying examinations. In a teaching hospital the attending physicians have finished their training and, more often than not, are subspecialists (having completed a fellowship).

Allopathic physicians spend many years learning about disease processes, procedures, laboratory tests, and imaging studies that can be used to diagnose diseases/disorders and a variety of therapies used as treatment. Ordering a test is not enough; one must also be able to interpret it rightly and apply it to the particular patient.

[12] Porter, *Cambridge*, 114.
[13] Ibid., 115.

For these reasons and more, medicine is called both a science and an art. Good clinical judgment, like bedside manner, is developed over time.

Early in my career I met "Mr. Green" (not his real name), a farmer. A few months before, he had had a heart valve replaced. The valve was working well, but Mr. Green had lost much weight and was found to have a serious infection, the treatment of which required weeks of hospitalization. After a few weeks Mr. Green was improving, and his appetite greatly increased. He began to regain weight and no longer appeared gaunt. By the time he was to be discharged to his home, his infection was cleared, and his skin glowed pink with health. I wanted to make sure he understood as much as possible about his condition, so I sat with him and reviewed his course. At the appropriate time I asked him, "Do you understand what kind of valve was placed in your heart? It is one that does not require you to be on anticoagulants, or blood thinners. It is a porcine valve."

"Porcine—what is that?" Mr. Green wanted to know.

"That means it came from a pig. It has been treated in certain ways to make it safe for you to have it, but originally it came from a pig."

Mr. Green's eyes widened with sudden understanding. He slapped his large farmer's hand on his overall-clad knee, and exclaimed, "Well, Doc, no wonder I eat so much!"

Mr. Green had indeed been eating large amounts of food but not because he had a pig valve in his chest. Mr. Green had been receiving steroids each day to prevent a reaction to the medication he was receiving for his fungal infection. His increased appetite was a side effect of the steroids. So, yes, Mr. Green was eating more and gaining weight. He also had a pig valve in his chest. But these two facts were not causally related.

The story of Mr. Green demonstrates, besides his fine sense of humor, the need for (1) accurate data and (2) correct interpretation of the data we have in medicine. For both of these to be present, Mr. Green needed information as well as interpretation. As his physician, I needed accurate data and the training to interpret the results. Another indispensable component of the physician-patient relationship is communication. Physicians and health-care professionals need to read and digest many books and much information.

Whatever else a patient may read, he/she needs to read the "book of self" and communicate the findings to those who provide care.

CBM: "The book of self" is an interesting concept. That means, among other things, that just as physicians and nurses have responsibilities in the healing relationship, so do patients. Patients must know themselves.

DJR: Each person who presents as a patient (and eventually, that is every one of us) knows best what it means to inhabit his or her own body. If there is pain, where it is, and how it feels. If a woman is a diabetic dependent on insulin, she will know how she feels when her glucose is 250 or perhaps 50. A person with arthritis knows when the pain is worse and which joints are apt to hurt. Whether it is "the usual," or a departure from the usual, the person who inhabits the body is best able to relate what is happening. These are symptoms, and they are communicated by the patient, in his/her history. The history is told by the patient and directed by the health-care professional's questions.[14] One caveat to remember is that communication includes not only what is said but also what is heard. Clarifying questions need to be included in the conversation. An example is, "What I understand you to be saying is . . .; do I have that correct?" Including such confirmatory questions is essential to good history taking from the physician's perspective.

After the history is reported, an examination is in order. The physician/health-care professional looks for signs. Signs are those things an observer can see or measure. When a patient reports pain, for example, the physician will look for swelling or bruising and pay attention to the color and temperature of the affected part. Those are all signs that help interpret the patient's symptoms.

Perhaps a young boy complains of leg pain after playing a baseball game. He will need to communicate (usually, as a result of questioning) whether his leg was hit by something or he fell or ran into something while moving. The doctor will examine the leg. Is it swollen? Bruised? Is there a red mark? Can the pulses in the leg be felt? These observations will be noted and compared with the story the patient tells.

---

[14] Emergency situations may differ from this scenario.

Perhaps an X-ray to look at the bone structure is in order. If the leg is red, hot, and swollen, some blood tests will probably need to be done. If the leg is cold and pulseless, other tests will be needed. Correct interpretation is a necessity for each of these. That depends on the competency of those who order the tests, those who complete them, and those who interpret them—a tall order but not impossible. The process begins with an accurate history, which is what the patient, with close questioning, provides. The next step is a competent physical examination followed by appropriate testing, accurately reported and interpreted. Then a plan of treatment can be developed and instituted. These are the usual ingredients needed for a good result.

CBM: All of that can be reassuring, but where does this leave the patient, the family member, the pastor, or a concerned friend when someone they know confronts the medical establishment? What can one who is not trained bring to the bedside of a patient?

DJR: They can bring several things. While I can recommend no single book or website to "get up to speed" in order to interact with medical personnel, that does not mean we are without resources. Bring your analytical mind, your reasoning power, with you when you face medical decisions. My father, a man who had little formal education, was advised by his cardiologist to have an internal defibrillator implanted. My father didn't know much at all about medicine, but he knew about mechanical things that needed power sources. Without a moment's hesitation he replied with his own question: "Doc, how long does the battery last in a thing like that?" Excellent question. My father was trying to make a major medical decision and wanted to know, if he went in that direction, how much time would pass before he would have to present his body again for a battery change.

Physicians may be able to answer your questions, but their time is usually limited, and their vocabulary is not always easily translatable. Communication depends less on how many words have been spoken than the amount of understanding that has occurred. When one is in doubt about what has been said, asking questions and clarifying terms is imperative. Repetition is also essential. Nurses and other health-care professionals are often excellent teachers. Try to communicate with every level/discipline in medicine, and do not be afraid to ask questions. Sometimes brochures have been prepared about frequently asked questions. These can be helpful, giving the reader information, which can be explained more fully by medical professionals. Some hospitals have excellent educational television channels to help patients learn more about their condition and its treatment. Whenever possible, become an active learner, even in the hospital.

The virtue of humility is necessary for everyone involved. Physicians and patients often differ significantly in their understanding of disease, disorder, diagnosis, and treatment. Questions asked and answered in a spirit of humility aid the process of understanding as little else can. Every discipline has its own vocabulary, and medicine is no exception.

Beyond these strategies the presence of an informal "advocate" is often of great help. My father had a major myocardial infarction (heart attack) and had coronary artery bypass graft (CABG) surgery immediately afterward. I spent as much time at the hospital as I could, helping him do his breathing exercises, keeping an eye on his progress, and translating the "medicalese" into words and terms he could understand. That relieved his physicians and nurses a bit and made my father, as well as my mother, more comfortable during a frightening time.

CBM: I know from personal experience, hospitalization can be stressful. Beyond health-care providers themselves, what help is out there for us and for our immediate family?

DJR: Extended family, friends, pastors, and other supports are much needed. On some occasions additional outside assistance is necessary. This is particularly true when disagreements arise between a patient or patient's family and the medical institution or staff about the plan of care or care itself, which cannot be resolved. Depending on the hospital, several mechanisms may be in place for helping aid communication and resolve dilemmas. Some hospitals employ patient advocates or patient representatives. A patient advocate acts as a liaison between the patient and his or her health-care providers. Generally these individuals have a great deal of experience that can be extremely helpful either in getting things done or in speaking up on behalf of the patient.

In 1992, the Joint Commission, the national accrediting agency for hospitals and nursing homes, mandated that any institution receiving Medicare and Medicaid funding must have in place a means for dealing with the ethical issues that arise in the health-care setting. By the year 2000, over 95 percent of hospitals had some sort of ethics committee or ethics consultation service. An ethics consultant will have training in ethics but not necessarily medicine, per se. That is, there is no requirement that the consultant be a physician or nurse (although many are), and many have a great deal of experience in the clinical setting. An ethics committee often includes members who represent medicine, nursing, clergy, the legal profession, social work, and the community. Depending on the hospital, an ethics consultation may be instigated by anyone involved with the patient in a hospital setting and may be requested by the patient or patient's family, as well. Usually a meeting is convened, the medical staff associated with the patient's care presents the problem to the committee (or consultant), and an effort is made to resolve the difficulty. The results are then presented to the patient and/or the family by the medical staff. Ethical dilemmas are often the result of a lack of good communication or communication skills on the part of some person(s). Taking the time to discuss the various aspects of the patient's care can help resolve the bulk of the issues that arise. When an impasse occurs, options for hospitalized patients are fairly limited to asking for a change in medical staff or changing institutions. These are not small matters, and they are not taken lightly.

Conclusion

In their effort to discern truth and make ethical decisions in the context of health care, Christians must read and interpret two books of revelation: the book of God and the book of nature. In fact, as historian of science Peter Harrison has argued, the rise of modern science is, at least in part, due to this realization.[15] God has made himself known in Scripture and in nature. He has revealed himself most emphatically in Jesus of Nazareth, the eternal Son of God in

---

[15] Peter Harrison, ed., *The Cambridge Companion to Science and Religion* (Cambridge: Cambridge University Press, 2010), 46–47. Harrison's complete argument can be found in his volume, *The Bible, Protestantism, and the Rise of Natural Science* (Cambridge: Cambridge University Press, 1998).

human flesh. Thus, in order to understand God's revelation most fully, we study both the Bible and nature, written revelation and created revelation. In medical science the book of nature includes the human body in all its stages of development from conception to natural death. When making decisions about life and death, we appeal to truth from both books.

Interpreting biblical texts in their context, paying attention to genre, grammar, and meaning, is crucial to understanding God's will. Likewise, interpreting symptoms, laboratory test results, and the medical vocabulary is important. At the end of the day, we affirm the coherence of truth; all truth is God's truth. Christians have nothing to fear from truthful science, and science has nothing to fear from faithful biblical interpretation.

We offer the following as a guide for making ethical decisions:

Process for Medical Ethical Decision Making

1. Define the ethical issue or problem.
2. Clarify the issue.
3. Pray for illumination by the Holy Spirit.
4. Glean the medical data on the issue:

   - What is the diagnosis?
   - What are the available treatments?
   - What are the possible outcomes?
   - Are there complications?
   - Are there implications for spouse, family members, or others?
   - What, precisely, is the moral question(s) to be answered?

5. Glean the scriptural data on the question, identifying the biblical issue:

   - Precepts or commands
   - Principles
   - Examples

6. Study the scriptural instruction carefully:

   - What does the text say?
   - What does the text mean?
   - What is the genre?

- What are the literary style and organization?
- What definitions and grammar are significant?
- What is the context?
- What are the overall theme, purpose, and historical significance?
- Apply the biblical instruction to formulate a potential answer.

7. Engage in dialogue with the Christian community.
8. Study the views of the church down through the ages.
9. Formulate a decision.

In this chapter we have discussed the translation of precepts and mores from ancient text to modern day. In the next chapter we take a look at a procedure (and an issue) that has ancient roots and remains controversial today. How does our ancient text inform our understanding of abortion?

Additional Resources

Hollinger, Dennis P. *Choosing the Good: Christian Ethics in a Complex World*. Grand Rapids, MI: Baker Academic, 2002.

Meilaender, Gilbert. *Bioethics: A Primer for Christians*. 3rd ed. Grand Rapids, MI: Eerdmans, 2013.

Pellegrino, Edmund, and David Thomasma. *The Christian Virtues in Medical Practice*. Washington, DC: Georgetown University Press, 1996.

Rae, Scott, and Paul Cox. *Bioethics: A Christian Approach in a Pluralistic Age*. Grand Rapids, MI: Eerdmans, 1999.

Part II

Taking Life

Chapter 3

The Sanctity of Human
Life and Abortion

Case: Oklahoma Mother Reportedly Refused
Cancer Treatment So Child Could Survive[1]

Stacie Crimm made the ultimate sacrifice—and she got her dying wish. As doctors and nurses wearing protective gear looked on last month, the 41-year-old mom got to hold her newborn daughter.

Three days later, Crimm died. But her baby girl, Dottie Mae, is alive, because her mom refused the cancer-fighting treatments that might have saved her life—and that she feared would risk the life of her unborn child.[2]

So begins the news report on Stacie Crimm of Ryan, Oklahoma, in October 2011. In March of that year, Ms. Crimm, a single woman, had learned she was pregnant. This was unanticipated, for she "had been told she would never be able

---

[1] "Oklahoma Mother Reportedly Refused Cancer Treatment So Child Could Survive," October 18, 2011, accessed December 3, 2013, http://www.foxnews.com/health/2011/10/18/oklahoma-mother-reportedly-refused-cancer-treatment-so-child-could-survive.

[2] Ibid.

45

to have children."[3] During her pregnancy, she sent text message after text message to her brother, Ray Phillips. Some of those described her headaches as well as double vision. She was worried that she might not live long enough to have the baby and asked Ray to take care of her child if she could not.

Ms. Crimm's fears had a basis in fact, as it turned out. In July she was diagnosed with head and neck cancer. She rejected chemotherapy because of its possible effects on the baby. Her tumor advanced, growing around her brainstem, where vital functions are regulated. Neither the baby nor the mother tolerated that, and the baby, at two pounds, one ounce, was delivered by C-section. The mother's desire to hold her baby was fulfilled, and later, as Ms. Crimm had asked him to do, Ray Phillips and his family took Dottie Mae to her new home.[4]

The story of Stacie Crimm highlights the decisions pregnant women with cancer face. Chemotherapeutic agents cross the placenta, meaning they affect the growing embryo or fetus. Early in the pregnancy this can cause malformations; later the effects can be intrauterine growth restriction, fetal toxicities, or stillbirth—and those are the effects on the developing child.[5] The mother has other effects to contend with, as well as facing the fact that her life may soon be over.

Questions for Reflection

1. What does *abortion* mean? Are there different categories of abortion, and if so, do the ethical questions change depending on what category of abortion is being considered?

2. Was Stacy Crimm obligated to forgo cancer treatment to preserve the life of her unborn baby? Or was it an act of supererogation (going above and beyond what duty demands)?

---

[3] Ibid.
[4] Ibid.
[5] G. Koren, N. Carey, R. Gagnon, C. Maxwell, I. Nulman, V. Senikas, and the Society of Obstetricians and Gynaecologists of Canada, "Cancer Chemotherapy and Pregnancy," *J. Obstet Gynaecol. Can.* 35, no. 3 (March 2013): 263–80, accessed October 31, 2013, http://www.ncbi.nlm.nih.gov/pubmed/23470115.

3. Under what circumstances, if any, can abortion be morally justified?

4. Do doctors have the moral authority to end the life of an unborn child?

5. What biblical norms or principles, if any, apply to medical technologies that did not exist when the Bible was written?

Discussion

C. Ben Mitchell (CBM): As we noted in our discussion of the Hippocratic tradition, questions about the morality of "taking human life" have been around for a long time. Early physicians were enjoined not to harm their patients. "I will give no deadly medicine to any one if asked, nor suggest any such counsel" the physician pledged, "and in like manner I will not give to a woman a pessary to produce abortion."

The subject of abortion may well be the most divisive moral fault line in contemporary culture. The controversy over abortion has raged in America and other countries at least since the 1960s. The Supreme Court's 1973 decisions in *Roe v. Wade* and *Doe v. Bolton* secured a place for the United States as the most permissive society in the world with respect to abortion laws and policy.

How has the abortion debate changed American medicine?

D. Joy Riley (DJR): Medicine has been dramatically impacted in ways both quantifiable and nonquantifiable by the Supreme Court decisions and the cultural upheaval that has followed. Before examining that impact, though, it is important to define our terms.

Abortion is "the termination of pregnancy, either spontaneously or intentionally, before the fetus develops sufficiently to survive. By convention, abortion is usually defined as pregnancy termination prior to 20 weeks' gestation or less than 500-g birthweight."[6]

---

[6] F. Gary Cunningham, Kenneth J. Leveno, Steven L. Bloom, John C. Hauth, Larry Gilstrap III, and Katharine D. Wenstrom, "Abortion," in *Williams Obstetrics*, 22nd ed. (New York: McGraw-Hill, 2005), 232.

(Note: one pound is 454 grams.) This is a medical definition; state laws impact the terminology as well.

CBM: The use of the term *abortion* in this text does not mean "miscarriage" or "spontaneous abortion." We will restrict the term to either medical or surgical abortions.

DJR: Yes, that helps limit the topic. We are addressing induced abortion: "the medical or surgical termination of pregnancy before the time of fetal viability."[7] Induced abortion can be described as:

1. elective (voluntary) abortion: "the interruption of pregnancy before viability at the request of the woman but not for reasons of impaired maternal health or fetal disease."[8]

2. therapeutic abortion: abortion to save the physical life or preserve the health of the mother, where "health" is defined as "all factors—physical, emotional, psychological, familial, and the woman's age—relevant to the well-being of the patient. All these factors may relate to health."[9]

Nancy Aries reviewed the abortion policy of the American College of Obstetricians and Gynecologists (an arm of the professional society for OB/GYN physicians) encompassing the years 1951–73. She reported that the organization dropped the term "therapeutic abortion" in 1970. According to her paper, this paved the way for the statement, "It is recognized that abortion may be performed at a patient's request, or upon a physician's recommendation."[10]

CBM: So the terms used for abortion were being changed in the early 1970s. That is not surprising given the cultural climate of the time. Beyond the definitions, we need to look at how abortions are performed. This is not in order to be graphic but so we

---

[7] Ibid., 241.

[8] Ibid., 242.

[9] *Doe v Bolton*, 1973.

[10] ACOG, "College Policy on Abortion and Sterilization," *ACOG Newsletter* 14 (September 1970): 2, quoted in Nancy Aries, "The American College of Obstetricians and Gynecologists and the Evolution of Abortion Policy, 1951–1973: The Politics of Science," *Am J Public Health* 93, no. 11 (November 2003): 1810–19.

understand what actually is going on during this procedure, or these procedures.

DJR: There are two primary types: medical and surgical. "Medical" refers to the administration of medications or drugs that, by differing mechanisms, cause the uterus to contract and expel its contents early. The drugs usually used for such abortions are mifepristone (an antiprogestin), misoprostol (a prostaglandin), or methotrexate (an antimetabolite). According to the (2001) American College of Obstetricians and Gynecologists (ACOG), a medical abortion is "an acceptable alternative to surgical abortion in appropriately selected women with pregnancies of less than 49 days' gestation."[11] A medical abortion requires (usually) two or more visits to the clinic or office by the patient and follow-up to make sure the pregnancy has been ended. Its attraction is the fact that anesthesia is not usually used.

Surgical abortions are done in a variety of ways, are usually accomplished in one visit, and may or may not use anesthesia. A surgical abortion requires either an appropriately dilated cervix (the opening of the uterus), or the removal of the fetus through the abdomen by hysterotomy (incision into the uterus) or hysterectomy (removal of uterus, and pregnancy, in this case).

Before fourteen to fifteen weeks, the cervix is expanded with dilators of increasing size inserted into the cervix via the vagina. The "contents of the womb" are mechanically removed, through vacuum aspiration or curettage (scraping of the uterus with a sharp instrument).

At sixteen weeks and beyond, a fetus is aborted by "dilatation and evacuation" or D&E. The cervix must be dilated widely; then the fetus is mechanically destroyed and removed. This is why pictures of aborted fetuses often show disconnected body parts. The placenta and any remaining tissue are removed by a "large-bore vacuum curette."[12]

"Selective reduction" can be offered when a woman is carrying multiple fetuses. It is done usually through the abdomen, at ten to thirteen weeks gestation. Under ultrasound guidance the abortionist injects potassium chloride (a salt) into the heart of the fetus(es)

---

[11] Cunningham et al., "Abortion," 245.
[12] Ibid., 243.

selected for reduction. The body of the fetus is usually reabsorbed into the mother's body.[13]

"Selective termination" is a similar procedure except it is done later in the pregnancy, after anomalies have been diagnosed. This procedure is "usually not performed unless the anomaly is severe but not lethal, meaning that the anomalous fetus would survive and require lifetime care, or the estimated risk of continuing the pregnancy is greater than the risk of the procedure."[14]

Another method, the "dilatation and extraction," or D&X procedure, also known as "partial birth abortion," was banned in the United States in 2003. Technically this procedure is described as one that "facilitates extraction and minimizes uterine or cervical injury from instruments or fetal bones."[15] The findings of the United States Congress cast a different light on the procedure:

> The Congress finds and declares the following: (1) A moral, medical, and ethical consensus exists that the practice of performing a partial-birth abortion—an abortion in which a physician deliberately and intentionally vaginally delivers a living, unborn child's body until either the entire baby's head is outside the body of the mother, or any part of the baby's trunk past the navel is outside the body of the mother and only the head remains inside the womb, for the purpose of performing an overt act (usually the puncturing of the back of the child's skull and removing the baby's brains) that the person knows will kill the partially delivered infant, performs this act, and then completes delivery of the dead infant—is a gruesome and inhumane procedure that is never medically necessary and should be prohibited.[16]

CBM: Thank you for clarifying terms for us. How has the abortion debate shaped contemporary medical education?

DJR: According to the standard obstetrics text used in medical schools, the first abortion law in the United States was enacted

---

[13] Cunningham et al., "Multifetal Gestation," in *Williams Obstetrics*, 941–42.

[14] Ibid., 942.

[15] Cunningham et al., "Abortion," 243.

[16] *Partial-Birth Ban Act of 2003*, accessed June 5, 2013, http://www.nrlc.org/abortion/pba/partial_birth_abortion_Ban_act_final_language.htm.

in Connecticut in 1821.[17] Although other states followed suit, therapeutic abortions, at this time primarily to save the life of the mother, remained legal in most states. That changed in 1973, with the *Roe v. Wade* and *Doe v. Bolton* decisions when abortion on demand became legal.

The Alan Guttmacher Institute, the polling arm of Planned Parenthood, reported the following data in 1979:

> From 1967 through 1978, approximately six million women obtained almost eight million legal abortions; about one in eight U.S. women of reproductive age has had a legal abortion. . . . More than 90% of abortions were performed in the first trimester by suction or sharp curettage. . . . Abortion rates in 1977 were highest for women 18–19 years old, for nonwhite and unmarried women, and for poor women eligible for Medicaid.[18]

Fast-forward to a report in 2009 of the American Congress of Obstetricians and Gynecologists (ACOG) Committee on Healthcare for Underserved Women. The committee reported 1.2 million abortions done in 2005, the lowest number since 1974. They noted that the majority of abortions were done by aspiration, although medical abortions were increasing. Furthermore, because of the decline in the number of abortion providers, the committee expressed concerned about access to abortion services. Apparently, in 1996, there were 2,042 abortion providers in the US. By 2005, that number had decreased to 1,787.[19] The ACOG committee expressed concern that women might not receive "comprehensive reproductive health services" because of the reduction in the number of abortion providers and the lack of mandatory abortion training in OB/GYN residencies.[20]

---

[17] Cunningham et al., "Abortion," 241.

[18] J. D. Forrest, E. Sullivan, and C. Tietze, "Abortion in the United States, 1977–1978," *Fam Plann Perspect* 11, no. 6 (November-December 1979): 329–41, accessed June 5, 2012, http://www.ncbi.nlm.nih.gov/pubmed/401078.

[19] American College of Obstetricians and Gynecologists, ACOG Committee Opinion No. 424, "Abortion Access and Training," *Obstet Gynecol* 113 (2009): 247–50, citing R. K. Jones, M. R. Zolna, S. K. Henshaw, and L. B. Finer, "Abortion in the United States: Incidence and Access to Services, 2005," *Perspect Sex Reprod Health* 40 (2008): 6–16, accessed June 5, 2012, http://www.acog.org/Resources_And_Publications/Committee_Opinions /Committee_on_Health_Care_for_Underserved_Women/Abortion_Access_and_Training.

[20] ACOG Committee Opinion No. 424, "Abortion Access and Training," 247–50.

In 2004, there were 252 OB/GYN residency programs in the United States. Of 185 which responded to a survey about abortion training:[21]

- 94 offered routine instruction in elective abortion.
- 72 made training in elective abortion optional.
- 19 provided no training in elective abortion.

My husband trained both in family practice and in obstetrics and gynecology. Instruction in abortion techniques was optional in his program, and he did not avail himself of it. Later, when he was setting up an OB/GYN practice, he was in need of surgical instruments. A retiring OB/GYN physician was selling his instruments, and we visited that physician in his home. He showed us his instruments, all displayed on a table for easy inspection. We saw some large dilators, and my husband commented on those. We thanked the physician and left. My husband could have used some of the instruments, but he did not buy them. What stopped him was the presence of those large dilators. Those dilators would be used in only one procedure, and that was a procedure my husband does not do: induced abortion, or "pregnancy termination." Induced abortion, or "pregnancy termination," although legal, is a moral dividing line, and the line exists in training as well as in practice.

That is why a number of OB/GYN doctors have formed the American Association of Pro-Life Obstetricians and Gynecologists (AAPLOG), now a 2,500-member special interest group within the American Congress of Obstetricians and Gynecologists. The organization notably came into existence in April 1973.[22] Their mission statement is as follows:

As members of AAPLOG we affirm:

1. That we, as physicians, are responsible for the care and well-being of both our pregnant woman patient and her unborn child.

---

[21] K. L. Eastwood, J. E. Kacmar, J. Steinauer, S. Weitzen, and L. A. Boardman, "Abortion Training in the United States Obstetrics and Gynecology Residency Programs," *Obstet Gynecol* 108, no. 2 (August 2006): 303–8, accessed June 5, 2012, http://www.ncbi.nlm.nih.gov/pubmed/16880299.

[22] American Association of Pro-Life Obstetricians and Gynecologists, "History of AAPLOG," accessed June 6, 2012, http://www.aaplog.org/about-2/history-of-aaplog.

2. That the unborn child is a human being from the time of fertilization.

3. That elective disruption/abortion of human life at any time from fertilization onward constitutes the willful destruction of an innocent human being, and that this procedure will have no place in our practice of the healing arts.

4. That we are committed to educate abortion-vulnerable patients, the general public, pregnancy center counselors, and our medical colleagues regarding the medical and psychological complications associated with induced abortion, as evidenced in the scientific literature.

5. That we are deeply concerned about the profound, adverse effects that elective abortion imposes, not just on the women, but also on the entire involved family, and on our society at large.[23]

While the AAPLOG stance may encourage us, the 2007 position of the ACOG Committee on Ethics will not. The latter published an opinion about physicians who refuse, on the basis of conscience, to provide abortions, contraceptives, or sterilization. That committee said such physicians should:

- Give patients prior notice of their moral commitments and provide accurate and unbiased information about reproductive services.

- Refer patients in a timely manner to another doctor who can provide the requested service.

- Provide medically indicated services in an emergency when referral is impossible or might affect a patient's physical or emotional health.

- Practice close to physicians who will provide legal services or ensure that referral processes are in place so that patient access is not impeded.[24]

Imagine being a physician of conscience today, caught in the cross-hairs of one's own professional organization. Where is one's source of stability?

---

[23] American Association of Pro-Life Obstetricians and Gynecologists, "Our Mission Statement," under "About Us," accessed June 6, 2012, http://www.aaplog.org/about-2.

[24] Kevin B. O'Reilly, "New ACOG Position on Abortion Refusal Drawing Fire," *amednews*, January 21, 2008, accessed January 28, 2014, http://www.amednews.com/article/20080121/profession/301219968/7.

Having surveyed a part of the medical landscape, it is time to establish a moral baseline with respect to human life. What does the Bible say about the nature of human life? What does it mean to be human? Who is included in the human community?

CBM: The Bible has a lot to say about our humanity. Furthermore, the history of Christian doctrine, especially the church's understanding of the person of the trinitarian God, provides a deep reservoir of teaching from which to draw. So let's begin there.

Both the Bible and the church affirm that Jesus of Nazareth is both fully God and fully human. What do we learn from the person of Jesus about what it means to be human? How does our Christology inform our anthropology? First, we learn from the physician Luke, among others, that Jesus was born of woman. Although his conception was miraculous, his gestation, as far as we know, was like that of all other human babies. For instance, we know his mother Mary carried him in her womb from conception to birth. There is no reason, then, not to assume that, like every other human being, Jesus began human life as an embryo. In addition, Luke informs us that the angel Gabriel told Mary to name her baby "Jesus" when she was only six months pregnant. Just as today, naming was an important ritual. Jesus seems to be treated as a person even before his birth. We know Mary was pregnant with Jesus when her cousin Elizabeth was six months pregnant with her son later known as John the Baptist. Again, except for the nature of his conception and his naming, Jesus' early development appears to be normal. Then we read, "While they were [in Bethlehem], the time came for her to give birth. Then she gave birth to her firstborn Son, and she wrapped Him snugly in cloth and laid Him in a feeding trough—because there was no room for them at the lodging place" (Luke 2:6–7).

So we can infer several important truths about human anthropology on the basis of biblical Christology. First, our humanity begins *in utero*. We are human beings from conception. This is not surprising given what we now know about genetics. We inherit twenty-three chromosomes from our mothers and twenty-three from our fathers. When those chromosomes combine through fertilization, at least one (twinning could occur) genetically unique human being is conceived. Second, we are embodied human beings from conception. That is, even though not fully developed, the early embryo is an organic, carbon-based, living human organism. Embodiment plays a central role in both Christology and anthropology since, like Jesus, from conception throughout eternity we will enjoy an embodied existence. There is no other way to be human than to be embodied. Among other things the church acknowledges Jesus' embodiment—and our own—each time we feast at the Lord's Table in Communion.

This anthropology is consistent with what the rest of Scripture teaches. When God created humanity, he made Adam "a living being" (Gen 2:7) with a material body (cf. Pss 90:3; 103:14). Human beings, *Homo sapiens*, were made in God's image and likeness (Gen 1:27). Although the Bible nowhere reveals precisely in what the image of God (*imago Dei*) consists, a number of possibilities have been offered historically. The *imago Dei* has been understood as (1) humankind's erect bodily form, (2) human dominion over nature, (3) human reason, (4) human prefallen righteousness, (5) human capacities, (6) the juxtaposition between man and woman, (7) responsible creaturehood and moral conformity to God, and (8) various composite views. One thing seems clear from Scripture, however; the *imago Dei* is not a "function" human beings perform so much as it is a "status" they enjoy.[25] The *imago Dei* is not what humans *do* but who humans *are*. This will become especially important as we discuss so-called marginal cases.

Moreover, the Bible teaches that human beings are unique among all other created beings. For instance, *only* human beings are imagers of God. We learn from Genesis 9, that being imagers of God brings unique obligations. Animals may kill and be killed for food (Gen 9:1–6a), but "whoever sheds man's blood, his blood will be shed by man, *for God made man in His image*" (Gen 9:6, emphasis added). Animals may be killed for human sustenance, but human beings may not be killed without just cause. Unjustifiable killing is a violation of the special dignity vested in human beings by God himself. The *imago Dei* is, therefore, the foundation of the doctrine of the sanctity, or sacredness, of every human life. In summary, every human life is to be received as a gift from the

---

[25] See C. Ben Mitchell, "The Audacity of the *Imago Dei*: The Legacy and Uncertain Future of Human Dignity," in Thomas Albert Howard, *Imago Dei: Human Dignity in Ecumenical Perspective* (Washington, DC: Catholic University Press of America, 2013), 79–112.

sovereign Creator, treated with reverence and respect, and should not be harmed without biblical justification.

DJR: The term *imago Dei* is not specifically defined by Scripture, but we discern the concept by careful reading and interpretation. Presuming it does so, how does Scripture speak about abortion?

CBM: The practice of abortion is not something new. We tend to think of obstetrics and gynecology as shiny new science, but people have been having babies for a long time. And, sadly, abortion is not new.

Old Testament Judaism prohibited abortion. Only one biblical text has been used to argue to the contrary, Exodus 21:22–25. There Moses is giving an interpretation of the laws about the treatment of slaves. In verse 22 he describes a case in which two men are fighting. In the course of their struggle, they accidentally hit a pregnant woman, causing harm to her unborn baby. Some texts interpret the harm as a miscarriage, others as a premature live birth. The way this argument goes is, if a miscarriage was the result of the fight and a fine (v. 23) not death (a life for a life) is required, then it seems clear that unborn human life does not have the same value as someone already born.

There are good textual reasons to understand Moses to be describing a premature live birth. First, the Hebrew word *yeled* is used for what comes from the womb following the fight. This word is never used except for a child who can live outside the womb. Another Hebrew word, *golem*, means "fetus" and is only used one time in the Old Testament (Ps 139:16). Furthermore, *yatza*, the verb that refers to what happened to the child after the injury to the mother, ordinarily refers to live births (Gen 25:26; 38:28–30; Job 3:11; 10:18; Jer 1:5; 20:18). The word normally used for miscarriage, *shakol*, is not used here (see Gen 31:38; Exod 23:26; Job 20:10; Hos 9:14). Finally, even if the text were referring to a miscarriage, it would not necessarily indicate that an unborn child is of less value than one who is already born. Note that this hypothetical case refers to an accident. The men did not mean to harm the child. Most societies, including ancient Jewish society, recognized that manslaughter should be distinguished from premeditated killing. This does not imply a distinction in the value of the life that was taken but in the culpability of the one who took the life. Wanton premeditation requires one sort of penalty, in this case, death; manslaughter, another. Cities of refuge were established (see Num 35:6) for those who committed less heinous crimes. More literal versions translate Exodus 21:22: "When men strive together and hit a pregnant woman, so that her children come out, but there is no harm, the one who hit her shall surely be fined" (ESV). Others interpret the meaning of the clause, "If people are fighting and hit a pregnant woman and she gives birth prematurely but there is no serious injury" (NIV).

In Psalm 139, David speaks vividly to the nature of unborn human life. In his lofty psalm David exults both in God's omniscience and omnipresence (vv. 1–12). In verse 13 he celebrates God's intricate involvement in his own fetal development: "For it was You who created my inward parts; You knit me together in my mother's womb." The word *kilyah* is used to refer to the "inward parts" (literally, reins or kidneys). In Hebrew poetry the inward parts were typically understood to be the seat of the affections, the hidden part of a person where grief may be experienced (Job 16:13), where the conscience exists (Ps 51:7), and where deep spiritual distress is sometimes felt (Ps 73:21). God formed David's deepest being. He wove his body or "colorfully embroidered" him in his mother's womb, so that he was "remarkably and wonderfully made" (Ps 139:14). In light of this reality, David's confession in Psalm 51:5 that he was a sinner from conception offers abundant testimony to his belief in personhood from conception since only persons can sin.

In Psalm 139:16, David refers to God observing "formless" substance. David uses the word *golem*—used only here in the Old Testament—to suggest that God's knowledge reached even to his earliest development *in utero*. No wonder the Hebrews found abortion and infanticide morally reprehensible.

Later in the history of God's people, God's judgment fell on those who killed the unborn. Elisha wept when he foresaw the crimes of the king of Syria who would "kill their young men with the sword. You will dash their little ones to pieces. You will rip open their pregnant women" (2 Kgs 8:12). And Amos prophesied against the Ammonites because they "ripped open the pregnant women of Gilead in order to enlarge their territory" (Amos 1:13).

These texts doubtless inform the noncanonical Jewish wisdom literature that further codified the Bible's view of abortion. *The Sentences of Pseudo-Phocylides* (c. 50 BC– AD 50) said, for instance, that "a woman should not destroy the unborn in her belly, nor after its birth throw it before the dogs and vultures as a prey." Included among the "wicked" in the apocalyptic *Sibylline Oracle* were women who "produce abortions and unlawfully cast their offspring away" and sorcerers who dispense abortion-causing drugs. Similarly, the apocryphal book, *1 Enoch* (first or second century BC), declared that an evil angel taught humans how to "smash the embryo in the womb." Finally, the first-century Jewish historian Josephus said, "The law orders all the offspring to be brought up, and forbids women either to cause abortion or to make away with the fetus."[26]

Contrast these injunctions with the barbarism of Roman culture. Cicero (106–43 BC) indicated that according to the Twelve Tables of Roman Law, "Deformed infants shall be killed" (*De Legibus* 3.8). Plutarch (c. AD 46–120) spoke of those whom he said "offered up their own children, and those who had no children would buy little ones from poor people and cut their throats as if they were so many lambs or young birds; meanwhile the mother stood by without a tear or moan" (*Moralia* 2.171D). According to an inscription at Delphi, because of the infanticide of female newborns, only 1 percent of 600 families had raised two daughters. European historian W. E. H. Lecky called infanticide "one of the deepest stains of the ancient civilizations."[27]

Against this horrific backdrop, the Hebrew doctrine of the "sanctity of human life" provided the moral framework for early Christian condemnation of abortion and infanticide. For instance, the *Didache* (c. AD 85–110), sometimes called "The Teachings of the Twelve Apostles," commanded, "Thou shalt not murder a child by abortion nor kill them when born." Another noncanonical early Christian text, the *Epistle of Barnabas* (c. AD 130), said, "You shall not abort a child nor, again, commit infanticide." Additional examples of Christian disapprobation of both infanticide and abortion can be multiplied. In fact, New Testament scholar Michael

---

[26] For these and other sources, see Michael Gorman, *Abortion and the Early Church: Christian, Jewish and Pagan Attitudes in the Greco-Roman World* (Downers Grove, IL: InterVarsity, 1982).

[27] W. E. H. Lecky, *History of European Morals: From Augustus to Charlemagne* (New York: Vanguard, 1927), 2:24.

Gorman has argued that the New Testament's silence on abortion is due to the fact that it was simply beyond the pale of early Christian practice.

Christians did not merely condemn abortion and infanticide, however; they provided alternatives, adopting children who were destined to be abandoned. For instance, Callistus (died c. 223) provided refuge to abandoned children by placing them in Christian homes. Benignus of Dijon (third century) offered nourishment and protection to abandoned children, including some with disabilities caused by failed abortions.

In summary, the witness of Scripture and the testimony of the early church are that every human being, from conception through natural death, is to be respected as an imager of God whose life has special dignity in virtue of his or her relationship to the Creator. Like the early church, Christians should be known as a people who protect, nurture, and cherish children as gifts from the Lord (Ps 127:3). Decisions about abortion—including the so-called "hard cases" (in the case of rape, incest, and to save the physical life of the mother)—must be made against this backdrop.

With this as background, could you bring us up-to-date on the history of abortion?

DJR: Abortion was "widely practiced" in antiquity, according to Gary B. Ferngren's *Medicine and Health Care in Early Christianity*. He states that the "fetus, being regarded as part of its mother, enjoyed no legal protection or absolute value until the third century, when abortion was penalized by a rescript issued under the emperors Septimius Severus and Caracalla between 198 and 211."[28] Christians and pagans disagreed about abortion, depending on their views of the fetus.

> Tertullian explicitly calls abortion homicide: "For us, indeed, as homicide is forbidden, it is not lawful to destroy what is conceived in the womb while the blood is still being formed into a man. To prevent being born is to accelerate homicide, nor does it make a difference whether you snatch away a soul which is born or destroy one being

---

[28] Gary B. Ferngren, *Medicine and Health Care in Early Christianity* (Baltimore: Johns Hopkins University Press, 2009), 101.

born. He who is man-to-be is man, as all fruit is now in the seed."[29]

Whether abortion was allowed by common law in the years 1200–1600 is a matter of some debate. It seems reasonable to say that abortion after the time of "quickening"—when the mother first feels the baby move within her—was not legal. Abortion and infanticide were punishable in the ecclesiastical courts during this time. After the Reformation the ecclesiastical courts were weakened, and royal jurisdiction filled the gap.[30]

Abortion was further restricted in Britain by Lord Ellenborough's Act of 1803. Among other provisions this act criminalized "pre-quickening" abortions.[31] "Instrumental abortion after quickening" was prohibited by Lord Lansdowne's Act in 1828.[32] The Medical Act in 1858 established a register of "qualified practitioners."[33] The danger to the pregnant woman's life posed by abortion in the 1800s seems to have been a substantial deterrent. By the end of that century, however, the number of abortions was increasing, apparently as a product of the desire to limit family size, as well as a result of the developments of anesthesia and antisepsis.[34]

More recent history reveals the macabre interplay between abortion, eugenics, and population control. In 1930, an American professor of obstetrics described the situation in Moscow, where public "abortaria" performed "fifty-seven abortions in one morning, with no anesthesia or sedatives. Initially abortions had been free, but so great was the demand that efforts were made to curb them. . . . Fear for women's health from repeated abortions . . . led to the law being tightened up, and eventually rescinded because of the effects on the population."[35] Though the law was rescinded, abortion remained legal for the purposes of eugenics, or to save the life of the mother.[36]

---

[29] Ibid.

[30] John Keown, *Abortion, Doctors and the Law* (Cambridge, UK: Cambridge University Press, 1988), 3–6.

[31] Ibid., 12–25.

[32] Ibid., 28.

[33] Ibid., 44.

[34] Ibid., 47.

[35] Ann Farmer, *By Their Fruits: Eugenics, Population Control, and the Abortion Campaign* (Washington, DC: The Catholic University of America Press, 2008), 108.

[36] "Decision of the Central Executive Committee and Council of People's Commissars of the USSR," *Moscow News*, July 8, 1936, cited in Farmer, *By Their Fruits*, 109.

These ideas were not bound by geographical locations. Dora Russell, active in the Abortion Law Reform Association and the birth control movement, "claimed that '[d]ogged persistence by women over many years has brought about abortion law reform in Britain.'"[37] She was married to the famous atheist philosopher Lord Bertrand Russell, who "warned against the racial deterioration of the European nations if 'the worst half of the population [became] the parents of more than half of the next generation.'"[38] Sweden's abortion laws were tied to their own sterilization laws. In 1937, it was recommended that "women be sterilized before abortion was granted, demonstrating that abortion functioned as a lure for sterilization."[39]

By 1967, Britain was ripe to pass the Abortion Act, which legalized abortions in the United Kingdom (with the exception of Northern Ireland) up to twenty-eight weeks' gestation. Abortions were legal when performed by registered practitioners and were provided free by the National Health Service. The US followed suit in legalizing abortion in 1973 but not by the voting public. The Supreme Court decided two cases in January of that year: *Roe v. Wade* and *Doe v. Bolton*. In *Doe*, the Court stated:

> We agree with the District Court . . . that the medical judgment may be exercised in the light of all factors—physical, emotional, psychological, familial, and the woman's age—relevant to the wellbeing of the patient. All these factors may relate to health. This allows the attending physician the room he needs to make his best medical judgment. And it is room that operates for the benefit, not the disadvantage, of the pregnant woman.[40]

Roe v. Wade and *Doe v. Bolton* based abortion on the liberty and privacy rights of the pregnant woman rather than the moral status of the unborn baby. A number of states have enacted legislation, or attempted with varying degrees of success, to counter this newfound right "discovered" by the Supreme Court. Examples

---

[37] Ibid., 62.

[38] Bertrand Russell, "Marriage and the Population Question," *International Journal of Ethics* 26, no. 4 (July 1916), in G. Greer, *Sex and Destiny: The Politics of Human Fertility* (London: Picador, 1984), 267, quoted in Farmer, *By Their Fruits*, 100.

[39] Farmer, *By Their Fruits*, 109.

[40] *Doe v. Bolton* (Blackmun 1973).

include requiring parental consent and notification for minors seeking abortions, mandatory counseling or wait times for the pregnant woman, and the provision of ultrasounds of the developing embryo/fetus.

CBM: Given the state of abortion in the United States today, how can Christians and churches respond?

DJR: For decades, the Catholic Church has led the way in protesting abortion and providing real help for women in crisis pregnancies. In recent years evangelicals have joined them, often as part of the twice-yearly "40 Days for Life" campaigns. This is a time of prayer, often in vigil near abortion clinics, with fasting, seeking an end to abortion on demand. Are the embryonic and fetal human beings the only ones of concern? Not at all. On the one hand, vulnerable humans are destroyed, and their mothers and families often struggle long-term afterwards.[41] Friends of mine struggle every year on anniversary dates of an abortion or the aborted baby's due date. On the other hand, those who work in abortion clinics also are affected, even if they are unaware. Reading Abby Johnson's story in *Unplanned*[42] gives an insider's view of the big business of abortion; transcripts of the Kermit Gosnell trial provide graphic details of what it was like to work in that environment.

Lila Rose is doing very important work in exposing some of the lies of abortion clinics. Her clandestine videography projects are shedding needed light in a dark world. To date the young president of Live Action has led projects aimed at exposing the willingness of "big abortion" to cover up sexual abuse, assist sex traffickers, and make false statements,[43] among other activities. Live Action's recent project, "Inhuman: Undercover in America's Late-Term Abortion Industry," is an accurate description of what goes on there, given the findings of the grand jury and the trial jury in the Kermit Gosnell case in Philadelphia.

---

[41] Wendy Williams and Ann Caldwell, *Empty Arms: Remembering the Unborn* (Chattanooga, TN: Living Ink, 2005).

[42] Abby Johnson with Cindy Lambert, *Unplanned: The Dramatic True Story of a Former Planned Parenthood Leader's Eye-Opening Journey Across the Lifeline* (Carol Stream, IL: Tyndale Momentum, 2011).

[43] "Live Action President Lila Rose," accessed May 24, 2013, http://www.liveaction.org/lilarose.

Kermit Gosnell was previously a licensed medical physician who "provided" late-term abortions in a poor section of West Philadelphia in a clinic ironically named "The Women's Medical Society." In February 2010, the clinic was raided by FBI agents, who thought they would find evidence of "prescription drug dealing."[44] What the agents found surprised them, it seems. According to the grand jury report:

> The clinic reeked of animal urine, courtesy of the cats that were allowed to roam (and defecate) freely. Furniture and blankets were stained with blood. Instruments were not properly sterilized. Disposable medical supplies were not disposed of; they were reused, over and over again. Medical equipment—such as the defibrillator, the EKG, the pulse oximeter, the blood pressure cuff—was generally broken; even when it worked, it wasn't used. The emergency exit was padlocked shut. And scattered throughout, in cabinets, in the basement, in a freezer, in jars and bags and plastic jugs, were fetal remains. It was a baby charnel house.[45]

Pennsylvania Attorney General R. Seth Williams was quoted in Gosnell's trial: "A doctor who with scissors cuts into the necks, severing the spinal cords of living, breathing babies who would survive with proper medical attention commits murder under the law. Regardless of one's feelings about abortion, whatever one's beliefs, that is the law."[46]

The jury agreed at least in part with the attorney general and the grand jury, finding Gosnell guilty of first-degree murder.

The Gosnell trial resulted in more than a guilty verdict for some of the charges against Kermit Gosnell. The trial also brought to light the horrible conditions and barbaric procedures often found in abortion clinics. While justice may have been served with the

---

[44] Enjoli Francis and Terry Morgan, "Abortion Doctor Kermit Gosnell Guilty of First Degree Murder," *ABC News*, May 13, 2013, accessed May 24, 2013, http://abcnews.go.com/US/gosnell-jury-deadlocked-counts-controversial-abortion-case/story?id=19168967#.UZ9j-YIpCKw.

[45] R. Seth Williams, district attorney, Report of the Grand Jury XXIII, First Judicial District of Pennsylvania, MISC. NO. 0009901-2008, January 14, 2011, accessed January 30, 2013, http://www.phila.gov/districtattorney/pdfs/grandjurywomensmedical.pdf.

[46] Mary Claire Dale and Patrick Walters, "Prosecutors Describe Philadelphia Abortion Clinic as 'House of Horrors,'" *cnsnews.com*, January 20, 2011, accessed May 24, 2013, http://cnsnews.com/news/article/prosecutors-describe-philadelphia-abortion-clinic-house-horrors.

guilty verdict, this is only one case in many. Is this systematic dis-
membering of our next generation really what we as a society wish
to embrace and subsidize? Is justice through the court system all we
can expect? What else can be done?

What can the church do about abortion? It is not enough to say,
"If you are against abortion, don't have one!" The church is called
to shine light in the darkness. The church needs to be the church:
repentant of sins and loving others into the kingdom. Here are
some practical ways to do that:

1. The church needs to get its own house in order. Strive for
   and encourage others in sexual purity. Encourage and build
   strong marriages and maintain intact families.
2. Come alongside those who are struggling, especially single
   parents and children in need of homes.
3. Pray, pray, pray.
4. Participate in some way in a "40 Days for Life" campaign.
5. Educate yourself about abortion; one place to begin is to
   watch the documentary "3801 Lancaster."[47]
6. Support local crisis pregnancy centers with your gifts of
   time, talent, and money.
7. Support those who are working to end abortion on demand,
   like

> Americans United for Life, http://www.aul.org
> Bioethics Defense Fund, http://bdfund.org
> Center for Bio-Ethical Reform, http://www.cbrinfo.org
> Live Action, http://www.liveaction.org
> Priests for Life, http://www.priestsforlife.org
> Right to Life, http://nrlc.org

Not all of these organizations (and this is far from a complete
list) will resonate with any one person, but a spectrum is available.
The point is this: it is not enough to expect someone else or some
other group to bear the responsibility of resisting this evil. Those
who are the church need to roll up their sleeves and participate in
shining the light into darkness, giving hope and help to those in
need.

"Those in need," the vulnerable in this life, are not only embryos,
fetuses, and newborns. "Those in need" can be any age and in any

[47] Available at http://3801lancaster.com, accessed June 4, 2013.

place. One particular place they can be found is at the other end of life's spectrum: approaching death. The next chapter addresses this important time of life. The concept of human dignity in dying is often talked about; what exactly does it mean?

Additional Resources

Beckwith, Francis J. *Defending Life: A Moral and Legal Case Against Abortion*. Cambridge: Cambridge University Press, 2007.

Best, Megan. *Fearfully and Wonderfully Made: Ethics and the Beginning of Human Life*. Sydney, Australia: Matthias Media, 2012.

Dunning, H. Ray. *Reflecting the Divine Image: Christian Ethics in Wesleyan Perspective*. Downers Grove, IL: InterVarsity, 1998.

George, Robert P., and Christopher Tollefsen. *Embryo: A Defense of Human Life*. New York: Doubleday, 2008.

Hoekema, Anthony A. *Created in God's Image*. Grand Rapids, MI: Eerdmans, 1986.

Jones, David Albert. *The Soul of the Embryo: An Enquiry into the Status of the Human Embryo in the Christian Tradition*. London and New York: Continuum, 2007.

Chapter 4

Human Dignity and Dying

Case: Who Has the Authority to
Remove Charles's Ventilator?

C harles, admitted two weeks ago, is fifty-one years old, has had multiple sclerosis for eight years, and has been disabled for four years from his job in auto tire sales. Until about six weeks prior to this admission, he was able to use his legs and get up on parallel bars. However, a recent exacerbation of his disease has caused difficulty speaking and talking, loss of use of his legs, and diminished use of his upper extremities. He was admitted with a staphylococcal pneumonia and on admission said he wanted full treatment. He quickly progressed to respiratory failure requiring intubation and ventilator assistance and to adult respiratory distress syndrome. At this point his caregivers in the intensive care unit (ICU) believe it is unlikely he will ever wean from the ventilator. He is currently stable, his infectious process is under control, and he is on 40 percent oxygen with relatively low ventilator settings. He responds appropriately to family members. There is a durable power of attorney (not a durable power of attorney for health care) form on the chart signed by the patient eight years ago naming his wife as his financial agent.

An ICU management meeting was held four days ago to discuss plans with his wife. She felt that he would choose, in light of his poor prognosis for improvement, to change to comfort care soon. The conclusion of the meeting was that a do-not-resuscitate order was written, but the current level of therapy would continue for another week and withdrawal of support would then be reconsidered. When his sister learned the next day that his wife planned to "pull the plug" soon, she became angry and said this would be "murder." In light of the tension between his wife and sister, his wife said she wanted to resign her role as surrogate.

His wife said that Charles was on a ventilator for a short time eight years ago and said clearly that it would be unacceptable for long-term use. In addition, he said he would not want to be admitted to a nursing home. At this point she believes he would consent to continuation of the ventilator for a few more days but that he would not want to go longer unless there were a 50 percent chance of weaning. His siblings agree that he would not want long-term vent support but believe it is too soon to quit, especially without an adequate weaning trial, and they would want to continue until there was a 95 percent change of nonweaning. Both sides verbalize strong antipathy toward the other with accusations about attitudes and motives.[1]

Questions for Reflection

1. Is it ever right to remove life-sustaining treatment like a ventilator?

2. How do we know what Charles would want in this case?

3. What is a durable power of attorney for health care? Who qualifies as a proxy decision maker?

4. How would you advise the family members of this patient?

---

[1] Case 4.07 in Robert D. Orr, *Medical Ethics and the Faith Factor: A Handbook for Clergy and Health-Care Professionals* (Grand Rapids, MI: Eerdmans, 2009), 88–89.

5. What biblical norms or principles, if any, need to be considered before making a decision in this case?

Discussion

C. Ben Mitchell (CBM): How would you like to die? Most people these days probably would say they want to die suddenly—quick and painlessly, maybe of a heart attack right after church. That would be a contemporary response to that question. For millennia, however, Christians thought a sudden death was a curse. "From a death that is sudden and unprepared for, deliver us, O Lord," was an ancient Christian prayer dating back to at least the third century. And in the Middle Ages the *Ars Moriendi* offered counsel to Christians about how to die well. Believers of the past took seriously the opportunity to prepare their hearts to go home to God. They also wanted to make things right with family, friends, and even enemies before they died. On reflection perhaps some preparation would be preferable.

Death seems to be a paradox in a number of ways. On the one hand, death is natural and everyone experiences it. Death affects 100 percent of the population. Sociobiologists tell us we are born to reproduce. After that, so they say, evolution has no use for us, and we begin the slow dying process. On the other hand, death is profoundly unnatural. When the "spark of life" is snuffed out, the body's drive toward homeostasis ceases, cells begin to decay immediately, and that which seemed so vibrant seems little more than a mannequin.

Likewise, death can appear to be a friend. Living things have a built-in senescence. As they age, they come increasingly closer to death. If the process is protracted and the body wracked by the debilitations of old age or effects of dementia, we often welcome death. Pneumonia is sometimes called "the old man's friend" because when the systems of the body just won't shut down on their own, pneumonia brings an end to life. And at the same time death is a profound enemy. Pain and suffering often attend our dying. Families are rent asunder through death. Hearts are broken and lives turned upside down by the sudden death of a child. Billions of dollars are spent annually trying to defeat this enemy.

What was your first experience with death and dying?

D. Joy Riley (DJR): My family was not shielded from death, and we attended wakes and funerals of loved ones with our extended family. My first experience with hospitals and dying occurred when I was in my early teens, visiting my grandmother in the hospital. We thought she was dying at the time. She was an Appalachian "mountain woman," unaccustomed to the ways of the more genteel. She was my father's mother, who had left her husband and children when my father, the baby of the family, was young. She had married again and had a daughter. My dad took our family to see her occasionally, and she visited in our home as well. His elder siblings had a less than warm relationship with their mother, however.

While we were in my grandmother's hospital room, she was moaning and crying out, saying something about her children. The nurse ushered us out of the room, saying, "She is confused." I wondered about the accuracy of that statement because she seemed to be asking God to forgive her for the harm she had caused her children. I obviously did not know the ways of the "genteel" either.

My first experience with patients came about slightly less than a decade later. Countless hours in college labs, dissecting formaldehyde-preserved animals, were followed by more hours in medical school gross anatomy labs, studying formaldehyde-preserved human body parts. On the heels of these classes was the class in professionalism. We had medical model patients—that is, people who were paid to pretend to be patients so we could examine healthy persons who could report on what we had done well and where we needed to improve. Then we practiced by examining real patients, but they were not "our patients," and we were not directly involved in their treatment. Obviously, physicians owe a debt of gratitude to a large number of people for their training.

In the third year of medical school, I had my first real, live patient. We'll call him Mr. Walton. It was our first day, and I was on the internal medicine service. Our resident stopped outside the patient's room, had us all don masks that covered our noses and mouths and gloves to cover our hands. "This man, Mr. Walton, will be your patient, Joy," he instructed me. That was followed by some laboratory data on the patient, and we filed into the room.

Great, I thought, *my first patient may well end my career if I contract TB* [tuberculosis] *from him.*

But I was wrong. The masks had startled me, and I had not processed correctly what I had heard. My first patient had *leukemia,* not TB. He had received chemotherapy, and his blood counts had dropped, so he was at risk of infection from me! He was also alone. No one had been able to reach his estranged daughter. He had no visitors, no flowers.

I really liked Mr. Walton. He endured his affliction without complaint. His mouth was raw because of the chemotherapy. Chemotherapy attacks quickly dividing cells, like cancer cells. The lining of the gut—from mouth to rectum—is also made of quickly dividing cells, but the chemotherapy could not tell the difference between those cells and cancer. Therefore, Mr. Walton's mouth and rest of his gut were sore and troubled. As his mouth improved, Mr. Walton wanted to eat again. What he really wanted was watermelon. He was disappointed that the hospital did not have watermelon on the menu. So I bought some at the grocery and brought him a few pieces in a thermos. My resident would not allow me to give it to him, however, because he was afraid it might have some bacteria that would sicken Mr. Walton. Something did make Mr. Walton sicker, and we started antibiotics and gave him some blood. Alas, our efforts were not enough, and Mr. Walton died. Shortly afterward, someone reached his estranged daughter, I learned. I never met her; more to the point, she and her father were not able to meet before he died. It was a sad case and not as rare as one would hope.

CBM: This case raises so many interesting questions about how we die. The shape of dying has changed dramatically since the invention of flexible plastic tubing (and other medical technologies of course). Prior to that, little could be done medically for those who were dying. Comfort care and pain medication were the only options. Today's medical technologies provide the means to extend human life span longer than ever before. Ironically, technology also often extends the dying process. Despite the fact that most people say they want to die at home surrounded by their families, more than half of us will likely die in a hospital surrounded by pumps, monitors, and, yes, flexible plastic tubing. According to one study, just over 25 percent of Americans die at home. Nearly as many die in a nursing home. The medicalization of death and dying has had an enormous impact on developed nations like the United States, Europe, and Japan.

DJR: In 1900 most people died at home; today, in the US, the situation is different.[2] In 2007 only 25 percent of us died at home, and 36 percent died while they were hospital inpatients. Five percent of those persons under sixty-five years and 28 percent of those sixty-five years or older died in nursing homes or long-term care facilities.[3]

I have thought about what people need at the end of life; after many years and experiences, I have come up with a relatively short list.

1. Being nourished
2. Being cherished
3. Being clean
4. Being comfortable
5. Being able and allowed to do the work of dying well

CBM: That is helpful. In a benchmark survey about what patients want at the end of life, 99 percent said they wanted to be able to name someone who could make decisions when they themselves could not; 93 percent wanted to have their financial affairs in order; 93 percent wanted to be able to say good-bye to important people; and 88 percent wanted to have a doctor who knew them as a whole person.[4] In cases like Mr. Walton's, where the family is estranged, presumably he would make his own decisions about treatment at

---

[2] David A. Fleming, MD, "Difficult Choices at the End of Life: A Personal Challenge for All Participants," *Missouri Medicine* 101, no. 6 (November/December 2004): 53.

[3] National Center for Health Making Statistics (US). Health, United States, 2010: With Special Feature on Death and Dying. Hyattsville (MD): National Center for Health Statistics (US); 2011 Feb. Special Feature on Death and Dying. Accessed January 31, 2014, http://www.ncbi.nlm.nih.gov/books/NBK54374.

[4] K. E. Steinhauser, N. A. Christakis, E. C. Clipp, et al., "Factors Considered Important at the End of Life by Patients, Family, Physicians, and Other Care Providers," *Journal of the American Medical Association* 284, no. 19 (2000): 2476–2482.

the end of life. But what if he cannot? What if he is either mentally impaired, unconscious, or in a coma?

DJR: First, we should not wait until we are in Mr. Walton's condition. We should talk to our loved ones now, while we are healthy, about what we want at the end of life. Do we prefer to die at home? What kind of funeral or memorial service do we want? Where do we want to be buried? Those are all important questions.

One area I could have added to my list of what people want at the end of life is "being in charge." Being in charge is important for most of us; yet the truth is, rarely are we truly in charge. That becomes clear to us when we have a schedule to meet, but our car refuses to start. It becomes even clearer to us, perhaps, in the hospital or when we are given a terminal diagnosis. It feels sometimes that anyone is in charge but we ourselves. Measures we can put in place, however, make our desires known to others in meaningful ways—ways that promote or even enforce those desires. Those measures are called "advance directives."

Advance (treatment) directives are written or oral declarations, by individuals capable of making informed and voluntary decisions, indicating preferences regarding future medical treatments. For example, patients may indicate a preference for or against certain medical interventions in specified clinical situations. Or they may specify surrogate decision-makers, in the event that they become incapacitated. The "living will," a durable power of attorney for health-care decisions, and "the will to live" are examples of advance directives.

The preferred advance directive is one that is written and signed by the individual (also called "principal"). The directive may declare that the person would like to be resuscitated in the event of a cardiac arrest; alternatively, the directive may state that the person does not wish to be resuscitated in the event of a cardiac arrest. There may be statements regarding the possibility of intubation (having a breathing tube inserted) and being placed on a ventilator; dialysis, in the event of renal (kidney) failure; or a variety of other possibilities. In fact, however, the potential scenarios are innumerable.

For this reason many people opt to designate a proxy decision maker. The document that permits this option is called a durable power of attorney for health care. It allows the author of the advance directive, instead of trying to anticipate all the possibilities and writing out the desired treatment plan for every eventuality, to choose a person to represent his or her interests in the event that he or she cannot make his or her own decisions. The important caveat here is that the surrogate (also referred to as "agent") is to make decisions based not on what he or she prefers but on what the principal, or originator of the directive—the patient—would desire. It therefore stands to reason that one needs to communicate clearly his or her desires and values about life and death to the person who will make those decisions.

One point especially should be emphasized about the durable power of attorney for health care. Through that document the agent or surrogate is empowered to make health-care decisions *only*. The agent cannot dictate who visits the patient in the hospital, how finances are used, or any other decisions besides health-care decisions. Even so, choosing a health-care agent or surrogate should be done thoughtfully. Likewise, to be entrusted with the health-care decisions of an incapacitated person is a heavy responsibility and one that should not be entered into lightly.

Finally, we all should get our documents and legal affairs in order now to help ease the pressures on our families during their time of grief. Doing so will be a much appreciated gift to them.

CBM: You used the expression, "doing the work of dying well." What do you mean?

DJR: Recently I had a conversation with a friend whose husband died a few months ago. She recalled those last days with him. He had been paraplegic for many years and was dying from a combination of problems. The treatment for one of his problems made the other condition worse. They knew it was only a matter of time. One day, in her usual manner, my friend was catching up her husband on family occurrences. He looked at her and held up his hand, signaling her to stop talking about those things. She astutely realized that he had "work to do," and she was interfering with that work of dying. She gave him the space he needed, sat with him, and talked when he wanted to talk. He died only a few days later, surrounded by those he loved. His family was able to release him and grieve well, in part because the husband/father had done the work he needed to do.

When I was in practice, I always took seriously the words of a patient who said, "I am going to die," or, "I will not be going home again," even if the evidence seemed to suggest otherwise. When a patient had a sense of impending death, I tried to do my work efficiently and well, making sure I had done all I could do but leaving as much time as possible for the patient to spend with his or her family. My work was important, but perhaps the most important work to be done was by the patient.

"Mr. R" was one such patient. He came into the hospital for a delicate operation to remove a tumor from his spinal cord. We assured him that his prognosis for recovery was good. Yet he repeatedly said he would never leave the hospital. He underwent several procedures during that hospitalization and did well. I stayed in contact with his family, and the time came for him to be discharged. His family was excited, and I was so pleased that he was going home after a trying time. But it was not to be. The nurses were helping him dress to go home when he suffered a cardiac arrest. We were unable to resuscitate him. Mr. R had been correct: he would not go home from the hospital. I learned much from Mr. R; perhaps the most important thing was to listen to the patient.

CBM: Indeed, listening to the patient is extraordinarily important when it comes to the experience of suffering.

To say that the problem of human suffering is one of the most incorrigible difficulties of our lived experience is to trivialize it. The problem of suffering and its close cousin, pain, raises the kind of questions that have kept many philosophers and theologians awake at night. More profoundly, the experience of suffering and its sometimes attendant pain has wracked the body and soul of mortals since the Adamic fall.

Tackling the problem of suffering is a daunting task. Who is equal to the task of explicating its nature, explaining its causes, and ameliorating its distress? I would like to offer the following discussion as a way of beginning our conversation on this topic. While I do not claim that my discussion is in any way comprehensive, I hope it will at least provide a suggestive treatment of the important aspects of a theology of suffering.

The Problem of Pain

Suffering may be painful and pain may cause suffering, but one is not identical with the other. Cornell University Medical College clinical professor Eric Cassell puts it, "Although pain and suffering are closely identified in the minds of most people and in the medical literature, they are phenomenologically distinct." It is difficult, if not impossible, to provide a satisfactory definition of pain. Pain is not something we define; it is something we feel, something we point to ("that hurts"), and something we sometimes fear. In her modern classic *The Body in Pain*, Elaine Scarry observes:

> For the person whose pain it is, it is "effortlessly" grasped (that is, even with the most heroic effort it cannot not be grasped); while for the person outside the sufferer's body, what is "effortless" is not grasping it (it is easy to remain wholly unaware of its existence; even with effort, one may remain in doubt about its existence or may retain the astonishing freedom of denying its existence; and finally, if with the best effort of sustained attention one successfully apprehends it, the aversiveness of the "it" one apprehends will only be a shadowy fraction of the actual "it"). For the person in pain, so incontestably and unnegotiably present is it that "having pain" may come to be thought of as the most vibrant example of what it is to "have certainty," while for the other person it is so elusive that "hearing about pain" may exist as the primary model of what it is "to have doubt." Thus pain comes unsharably into our midst as at once that which cannot be denied and that which cannot be confirmed.[5]

Pain is an interior state of consciousness. Whether physical or psychical, it hurts, it aches, it burns, it crushes, it throbs, it pounds, it sears, it stabs. Moreover, pain is idiosyncratic. Despite my best efforts, I cannot "feel your pain" or know how your pain feels. I might be able to discuss it by analogy (does it feel like a headache in your leg?). I might be able to approximate its intensity (does it hurt worse than burning your finger on a match?). I might be able to quantify its duration (has it hurt for more than a week?).

---

[5] Elaine Scarry, *The Body in Pain: The Making and Unmaking of the World* (New York: Oxford University Press, 1987), 4.

Nevertheless, pain is a singularly personal, subjective experience, known fully only by the one who is experiencing it.

Evidence suggests that we are doing a better job than ever in controlling pain. According to several studies, in approximately 90 percent of cancer patients, pain can be controlled through relatively simple means. Moreover, a consensus statement from the National Cancer Institute Workshop on Cancer Pain concluded that "every patient with cancer should have the expectation of pain control as an integral aspect of his/her care throughout the course of the disease."[6] In fact, says Edmund Pellegrino, "With the optimum and judicious use of [pain management techniques], there are virtually no patients whose pain cannot be relieved."[7] Yet there is a difference between pain and suffering. Anyone who has ever gotten a paper cut knows that it hurts, but hardly anyone seriously says he or she "suffers" from a paper cut. While childbirth, I'm told, can be immensely painful, few new mothers describe their ordeal as suffering.

DJR: As you point out, although pain and suffering are related, they are not the same. One cannot be a philosopher without contemplating suffering, and it seems that the certainties of life (such as death and taxes) should probably include suffering as well. What that means can fill volumes, and it has. Can you distill some of the more important aspects of suffering into a few pages?

CBM: Let's begin with the nature of suffering. Eric Cassell argues that pain grows closer to suffering when: (1) the pain is so severe it is virtually overwhelming, (2) the patient does not believe the pain can be controlled, and (3) the pain continues for a long time so the pain seems to be endless. "In sum," he says, "people in pain frequently report suffering from pain when they feel out of control, when the pain is overwhelming, when the source of the pain is unknown, when the meaning of the pain is dire, or when the pain is apparently without end."[8]

---

[6] US Department of Health and Human Services, *Management of Cancer Pain*, Clinical Practice Guideline, Number 9 (1994), Section 1.1.

[7] Edmund Pellegrino, "The False Promise of Beneficent Killing," in *Regulating How We Die: The Ethical, Medical, and Legal Issues Surrounding Physician-Assisted Suicide,* ed. Linda L. Emanuel (Cambridge, MA: Harvard University Press, 1998), 73.

[8] Eric J. Cassell, *The Nature of Suffering and the Goals of Medicine* (New York: Oxford University Press, 1991), 35.

As with pain, "the only way to learn whether suffering is present is to ask the sufferer."[9] Suffering may take many forms, from psychological to social and from spiritual to political. What seems to be a defining characteristic of suffering is that it violates one's integrity as a person. The self is fragmented, unraveled, and imploded by suffering. Consider the suffering of Job who laments:

> I am disgusted with my life.
> I will express my complaint
> and speak in the bitterness of my soul.
> I will say to God:
> "Do not declare me guilty!
> Let me know why You persecute me.
> Is it good for You to oppress,
> to reject the work of Your hands,
> and favor the plans of the wicked? . . .
> Your hands shaped me and formed me.
> Will You now turn and destroy me?
> Please remember that You formed me like clay.
> Will You now return me to dust?
> Did You not pour me out like milk
> and curdle me like cheese?" (Job 10:1–3, 8–10)

Or one hears the anguish of the psalmist in Psalm 88:

> Lord, God of my salvation,
> I cry out before You day and night.
> May my prayer reach Your presence;
> listen to my cry.
> For I have had enough troubles,
> and my life is near Sheol.
> I am counted among those going down to the Pit.
> I am like a man without strength,
> abandoned among the dead.
> I am like the slain lying in the grave,
> whom You no longer remember,
> and who are cut off from Your care. (Ps 88:1–5)

Even when unrelated to illness or disease, suffering may still ravage the person of the sufferer. William Nicholson's play,

---

[9] Scarry, *The Body in Pain*, 42.

Shadowlands, movingly portrays the nearly inexpressible suffering of C. S. Lewis after the death of his beloved wife, Joy:

> No shadows here. Only darkness, and silence, and the pain that cries like a child. It ends, like all affairs of the heart, with exhaustion. Only so much pain is possible. Then, rest.
> So it comes about that, when I am quiet, she returns to me. There she is, in my mind, my memory, coming towards me and I love her again as I did before, even though I know I will lose her again, and be hurt again.[10]

One wonders how Lewis's masterful theodicy, *The Problem of Pain*,[11] might have been altered had it been written after 1960, the year Joy died, rather than in 1940. Two years after her death, Lewis wrote to his good friend, Sheldon Vanauken, "I am now as convalescent as (apparently) I am ever likely to be. Loneliness increases as health returns. One must have the capacity for happiness in order to be fully aware of its absence."[12] The most severe form of suffering may be deprivation of one's person from other persons.

Suffering, moreover, does not arise ex nihilo. One always suffers from something. The unraveling is due to some experience, some pathology, some dementia. Thus, it is appropriate to speak of suffering from moral evil, material circumstances, or some combination of the two. Daniel Sulmasy is Kilbride-Clinton Professor of Medicine and Ethics in the Department of Medicine and Divinity School at the University of Chicago. His taxonomy of suffering is a helpful matrix by which to classify types of suffering.[13]

Taxonomy of Suffering

Type I. Human beings can suffer as a result of our own moral evil without any intervening material occasion; examples include the pangs of conscience, remorse, and guilt. This is the experience of personal moral finitude. A physician may feel guilty about having

[10] William Nicholson, *Shadowlands* (New York: Samuel French, Inc., 1990), 101.
[11] C. S. Lewis, *The Problem of Pain* (San Francisco: HarperOne, 2009).
[12] Letter from Lewis to Vanauken, June 30, 1962, in C. S. Lewis, *The Collected Letters of C. S. Lewis*, vol. 3: *Narnia, Cambridge, and Joy, 1950–1963* (San Francisco: HarperCollins, 2007), 1354.
[13] Daniel P. Sulmasy, "Finitude, Freedom, and Suffering," in *Pain Seeking Understanding: Suffering Medicine, and Faith,* ed. Margaret E. Mohrmann and Mark J. Hanson (Cleveland, OH: Pilgrim, 1999), 94–95.

abandoned a patient and recognize his or her limited individual capacity for good. In penance we confess our moral finitude as undermining our intrinsic dignity.

Type II. Human beings can suffer as a result of the moral evil of others without any intervening material occasion; examples include experiences of loneliness, hurt, and alienation. This is the experience of the moral finitude of others. If one were a patient, one might feel hurt by the cold and relatively inattentive manner in which one was treated by one's physician. No material wound or blow need serve as an intervening occasion of the suffering; the moral failure of the physician is sufficient cause. One recognizes that the world's love is finite.

Type III. Human beings can suffer as a result of the moral evil of self or of others mediated through material occasions of suffering. The long and horrible list of examples includes self-mutilation, torture, assault, rape, poisoning, murder, war, and willful negligence. These are at once experiences of the moral finitude of others and of the material finitude of one's own person. Records and memories of "experiments" performed on Nazi prisoners provide especially egregious medical examples. More subtly, a physician's greed may lead to excessive use of medical technologies with attendant physical harm to some patients.

Type IV. A myriad of material occasions of human suffering require no moral evil whatsoever—the central problems of medical suffering. Examples include fractured bones that result from landslides, inherited diseases like cystic fibrosis and hemophilia, and the relentless commonplaces such as arthritis, diabetes, cancer, heart attacks, and strokes. These are personal experiences of material finitude. From the physician's perspective they can also represent the physician's own experience of the finitude of medicine. Medicine does not grant immortality.

Mixed Types. Certainly occasions of suffering can be, in part, directly material and, in part, the result of moral evil. Multiple combinations and permutations are possible. Examples could include a person with lung cancer who had a genetic predisposition but who also started smoking at an early age, in part because greedy tobacco company executives, motivated by a desire for profits, deliberately repressed evidence about the addictive nature of cigarettes and authorized an advertising campaign aimed at teenagers. The bad genes are a contributing factor, but the teenager's decision to smoke and the business practices of the tobacco company played significant roles also. This taxonomy is admittedly artificial. Suffering is, more often than not, impossible to dissect with such precision. Nevertheless, this taxonomy helps us locate suffering within its moral and material matrices.

DJR: Understanding the different kinds of suffering is one thing, and the rubric you have presented is helpful. Yet most of us grapple not with how to define it but how to understand it, if that is possible. Why? is a common question. What help can you give us?

CBM: A theology of suffering must begin with the assertion that this is not the way things are supposed to be.

Making Sense Out of Suffering

To make sense out of suffering is, first, to realize that suffering is a result of human sin; it is a consequence of the Adamic fall. Had our first parents obeyed God, there would have been no suffering. Because of the disobedience of our progenitors, humanity was destined to be bruised and bloodied. Because our first parents refused God's way, a chain of events was set in motion that culminated in a curse. "The ground is cursed because of you. You will eat from it by means of painful labor all the days of your life. It will produce thorns and thistles for you, and you will eat the plants of the field. You will eat bread by the sweat of your brow until you return to the ground, since you were taken from it. For you are dust, and you will return to dust" (Gen 3:17–19). Philosopher Peter Kreeft puts it simply but profoundly when he says, "All three evils, sin and death and suffering, are from us, not from God; from our misuse of our free will, from our disobedience. We started it!"[14]

---

[14] Peter Kreeft, *Making Sense Out of Suffering* (Cincinnati, OH: Servant Books, 1986), 116.

In light of the fact that human beings are by nature opposed to God and God's way, the real question to be asked in the face of suffering is not "Why me?" but "Why not me?" The consequences of the fall into sin being what they are, any day without suffering is a day of grace and mercy. This may seem like thin gruel when the experience of suffering is at its apex, but we must embrace the reality of post-Adamic suffering as part of the groundwork of our world-view. Sadly the contemporary theological naivete of Christians and non-Christians alike has left them without an answer to the problem of sickness, suffering, or death in the world. When suffering comes—and for the overwhelming majority of Adam's race it will come—contemporary individuals have no philosophical category or worldview through which to interpret it. If one begins with the assumption that suffering is endemic to the human condition, then there can be no such thing as "pointless" suffering. This is not to argue that suffering is to be sought but that suffering is deserved. God is just in allowing suffering. In other words, the important question is not, Why do bad things happen to good people? But, Why do good things happen to bad people?

A second assumption necessary to make sense out of suffering is that suffering may have redemptive purposes or good ends. This is not the view that suffering is good in and of itself. It is astounding how many Christians naively cite Nietzsche's axiom: "That which does not kill us makes us stronger." Suffering is not good, but suffering may have good consequences. C. S. Lewis calls suffering "God's megaphone," by which he means it calls us back to the Creator and announces our dependence on the one who made us. Says Lewis:

> Now the proper good of a creature is to surrender itself to its Creator—to enact intellectually, volitionally, and emotionally, that relationship which is given in the mere fact of its being a creature. When it does so, it is good and happy. Lest we should think this is a hardship, this kind of good begins on a level far above the creatures, for God Himself, as Son, from all eternity renders back to God as Father by filial obedience the being which the Father by paternal love eternally generates in the Son. This is the pattern which man was made to imitate—and wherever the will conferred by the Creator is thus perfectly offered back

in the delighted and delighting obedience by the creature there, most undoubtedly, is Heaven, and there the Holy Ghost proceeds. In the world as we know it, the problem is how to recover self-surrender. We are not merely imperfect creatures who must be improved: we are, as John Henry Newman said, rebels who must lay down our arms. The first answer, then, to the question why our cure should be painful, is that to render back the will which we have so long claimed for our own, is in itself, wherever and how-ever it is done, a grievous pain.[15]

Suffering, therefore, calls us to surrender our will to God's. Against the backdrop of our rebellion and its consequences, this must be seen ultimately as a good.

Third, in order to make sense of suffering, we must see it as an important component in the development of our sense of com-passion and identification of community. In Stanley Hauerwas's essay on suffering in his provocative volume *Suffering Presence*, he observes that "it is our capacity to feel grief and to identify with the misfortune of others which is the basis for our ability to recognize our fellow humanity."[16] Only human beings experience genuine suffering. In a dark but real sense, suffering unites the human com-munity. Animal pain is real; we ought not unnecessarily to harm animals, but they do not suffer in the same sense in which persons suffer. Sulmasy makes this point clear by defining suffering as "the experience of finitude in tension with intrinsic human dignity."[17] Since animals do not share the "intrinsic dignity" of human beings, they experience no such tension and, thus, no suffering in this sense. This observation may help us interpret the permission in Genesis 9:1–6 to kill animals for food at the same time premedi-tated homicide is both strictly forbidden and penalized.

Finally, a theology of suffering must be informed by the reality that this is not the way it will always be. The more one suffers, the more one can identify with the apostle Paul's hopeful lament

---

[15] Lewis, *The Problem of Pain*, 90–91.

[16] Stanley Hauerwas, *Suffering Presence* (South Bend, IN: University of Notre Dame Press, 1986), 25.

[17] Daniel P. Sulmasy, "Finitude, Freedom, and Suffering," in Margaret E. Mohrmann and Mark J. Hanson, eds., *Pain Seeking Understanding: Suffering, Medicine, and Faith* (Cleveland, OH: Pilgrim, 1999), 94–95.

(which is not an oxymoron) in 2 Corinthians 4–5: "Even though our outer person is being destroyed, our inner person is being renewed day by day" (4:16). The body is perishing. Sometimes it is perishing so palpably as to call the experience suffering. "Indeed," says Paul, "we groan" (5:2). Sufferers know groaning. But for those who know the Suffering Savior, we shall not always groan. For, as Paul says, we confidently await the day when "mortality may be swallowed up by life" (5:4). We may also appeal to 1 Peter in order to understand this point. To a people experiencing terrible suffering and almost unspeakable dislocation, Peter says:

> Praise the God and Father of our Lord Jesus Christ. According to His great mercy, He has given us a new birth into a living hope through the resurrection of Jesus Christ from the dead and into an inheritance that is imperishable, uncorrupted, and unfading, kept in heaven for you. You are being protected by God's power through faith for a salvation that is ready to be revealed in the last time. You rejoice in this, though now for a short time you have had to struggle in various trials. (1 Pet 1:3–6)

Suffering cannot be interpreted or understood apart from these realities. To respond appropriately to suffering, we must renew our affirmation of these verities. Without coming to grips with these truths, we will be able to help neither ourselves nor others.

DJR: What, then? If suffering can result in good, what is a proper response of those witnessing the suffering of others?

CBM: The Bible offers insights to this, certainly, and we will turn to those now.

Relieving Suffering

Suffering becomes unbearable when we are hopeless and alone. Job expresses this morbid fact when, in the darkness of the moment of suffering, he cries, "For He is not a man like me, that I can answer Him, that we can take each other to court. There is no one to judge between us, to lay his hand on both of us. Let Him take His rod away from me so His terror will no longer frighten me. Then I would speak and not fear Him. But that is not the case; I am on my own" (Job 9:32–35).

The church holds three offices or functions in the world. The church has a prophetic office, a priestly office, and a kingly office. When the church functions obediently with respect to suffering, the church herself can provide a context in which suffering can be experienced in ways that help make sense of that experience.

First, in her prophetic office, the church calls her members to understand and follow the way of the Lord Jesus. In holiness and obedience the church will affirm the theology of suffering, embracing its reality and anticipating its relief. Second, in her priestly office, the church will engage in comprehensive ministry to those who are suffering. To rescue the perishing and care for the dying means the church will come alongside those who are suffering, provide compassionate ministry to the dying, and point persons to the hope of the Christian's inheritance. Finally, in her kingly ministry, the church will offer protection against the evils of the age, including the culture of death and its embrace of assisted death.

Relief of suffering must not be offered through relieving the sufferer of life itself. It is more than strange; it is a decided evil to remove what Sulmasy calls "the experience of finitude in tension with intrinsic human dignity"[18] by assaulting that dignity through premeditated homicide.

Edmund Pellegrino insightfully said:

> Seriously ill persons suffer commonly from alienation, guilt, and feelings of unworthiness. They often perceive themselves, and are perceived by others, as economic, social, and emotional burdens. They are exquisitely susceptible to even the most subtle suggestion by physician, nurse, or family member that reinforces their guilt, shame, or sense of unworthiness.
>
> It takes as much courage to resist these subliminal confirmations of alienation as to withstand the physical ravages of the disease. Much of the suffering of dying patients comes from being subtly treated as nonpersons. The decision to seek euthanasia is often an indictment against those

---

[18] Sulmasy, "Finitude, Freedom, and Suffering," 92.

who treat or care for the patient. If the emotional impediments are removed, and pain is properly relieved, there is evidence that many would not choose euthanasia.[19]

To halt the assisted-death juggernaut, the church may have to reestablish her threefold ministry as prophet, priest, and king. That may mean, among other things, that churches will once again have to found hospitals and fund hospices where dying patients are treated with compassion and dignity, not prematurely dispatched. God help us if we do not rise to the challenge.

Let's return to being nourished, cherished, clean, comfortable, and dying well. Those are helpful topics.

Being Nourished

DJR: Being nourished is usually not too difficult if one's alimentary canal (gastrointestinal tract) is working well and one can chew and swallow food. When the person has a problem with those functions, however, feeding is a challenge. It should not be surprising, then, that feeding issues, also called "artificially administered nutrition and hydration," have figured prominently in the public debate about end of life in our society.

What are the possibilities? If chewing, swallowing, and the GI tract all work, feed the patient! Unless, that is, the GI tract is about the only thing that works. One might hear a doctor or nurse say, "We seem to be feeding the tumor more than your mother." If that is the case, then the decision has to be about whether one is feeding the patient or only prolonging her dying. This is especially true if the patient is being cajoled and pressured into eating when she has no interest in doing so. These kinds of considerations should be evaluated by the medical team and the patient. If she is unable to make those decisions herself, her family or proxy decision maker may be brought into the process.

If chewing does not work well, the diet may be changed from solid to soft food. My mother-in-law had to have all of her teeth extracted, and her dementia was advancing. Pureed foods made it possible to hand-feed her for the rest of her years. Hand-feeding can work with other diets besides pureed ones, and a variety of

---

[19] Edmund D. Pellegrino, "Doctors Must Not Kill," *The Journal of Clinical Ethics* 3 (Summer 1992), 96–97.

personnel is usually available to help with dietary concerns. Consulting with someone from the speech therapy (also called speech pathology) or nutrition departments is an excellent idea for a patient with feeding difficulties. Usually the physician will initiate a consultation with the appropriate personnel.

Sometimes hand-feeding is impossible, however. Perhaps the patient has had a stroke and cannot chew or cannot swallow. Alternatively, the patient may have a problem with the jaw, mouth, esophagus, or other structures that makes chewing or swallowing problematic or impossible for some period of time. In those cases feeding tubes may become a subject of discussion. There are several kinds:

Nasogastric tube (NG tube)—goes from the nose into the stomach through the esophagus: these are usually short-term solutions, lasting up to several weeks.

Nasojejunostomy tube (N-J tube)—rarely used, this tube enters through the nose also, and extends to the jejunum, the second portion of the small intestine.

Gastrostomy tube (G-tube or PEG)—surgically placed, this tube goes through the abdominal wall to deliver a liquid-food mixture into the stomach.

Jejunostomy tube (J-tube)—also surgically placed, this tube delivers a liquid-food mixture into the jejunum.

Total parenteral nutrition (TPN)—If the bowel doesn't work well, yet another methodology may be employed in some instances. This method is also a tube, and it is used to administer nutritive substances, but it is not a feeding tube. A liquid providing both nutrition and fluids is administered through intravenous (IV) tubing, into a major (large) blood vessel through a surgically installed port, or place of access. TPN is occasionally indicated for those who are on bowel rest for a variety of reasons, such as recent extensive bowel surgery, advanced bowel disease, and a few other indications.

All feeding includes risks, such as risks of choking and aspiration (having food go into the lungs) from both hand-feeding and tubes inserted into the stomach. Caregivers must constantly guard against aspiration. Furthermore, many patients experience irritation from a tube placed through the nose and will often pull them out. The tube is usually reinserted, and sometimes restraints or sedation for the patient are recommended to avoid repeated tube removal. Any surgical placement of a tube incurs the usual surgical risks, as well as those associated with the particular area of placement. Surgical risks typically include bleeding, infection, numbness in the area of incision, and death (from a variety of causes). When a tube is placed through the wall of the abdomen, some other risks are entailed. Unintended perforation of (making a hole in) either a loop of bowel or a blood vessel are only two of a number of possible complications.

These are some of the issues involved in being nourished; we turn now to the next concern.

Being Cherished

To cherish someone is to hold them dear; treat them with affection, or care for them tenderly. This is not part of any medical care plan, but it is the role of family and friends. To that end medicine can make provision for that in its visitation hours and policies. Sometimes the most important "activity" a patient in a hospital can do is to rest, and policies need to allow for that to occur, too.

A wealthy woman, who had little experience with hospitals, was admitted to the ICU one night. Her condition was stabilized, and tests were completed. A friend thoughtfully brought by some scented soaps, which the nurses used when bathing her. It did not take away the bad news of her terminal diagnosis, but she felt cared for, as evidenced by her gratitude expressed to the staff.

Being Clean

Bathing the patient is typically a nursing or ancillary staff duty. It is included here because of its importance to the patient. Sometimes it is far more important than we know. Two brothers, very poor, were brought to the medical center with a contagious skin infection. The first order written was "bathe the patient"; antibiotics would certainly not be enough if the skin was not cleansed.

Being clean applies not only to the outside. Those who are dying often want, like my grandmother earlier described, to be forgiven of the wrongs they have done. Their illness or condition may be aggravated by a heavy heart, a weighted conscience. Many family members, perhaps long estranged, have been called to the bedside of a dying relative. That bedside visit is a golden opportunity for needed communication. In addition to family or friends being called to the bedside, patients often need pastoral counsel, although this may not be recognized by the medical personnel.

CBM: Given the strict regulations in place regarding privacy of patient information, how do pastors and priests learn of their congregants or parishioners being hospitalized?

DJR: That is an important point. If the patient is able, he or she needs to let the pastor/priest know of the hospitalization. Otherwise, a family member or friend can inform the spiritual leader. The medical or nursing staff can ask the patient if someone needs to be notified, but they are restricted regarding the transfer of patient information.

Being Comfortable

Sadly hospitals and comfort do not always go together, but they can. The indignities suffered through the poking and prodding and those indecent gowns are real, but people who become patients can be made, to varying degrees, comfortable.

Explanation—I saw the chart note our referring orthodontist had written to the orthodontist in our new town. It said, "Great kid, great mom. Explain, explain, explain." I suspect I remember why he wrote that. Perhaps it was because our son vomited on the referring orthodontist—and his shoes—during a morning appointment. I had not considered the consequences of feeding a child breakfast before a dental appointment, and no one had thought to explain to me that my child had a prominent gag reflex.

A patient in a doctor's office or the hospital faces many unknowns. Explanation can go a long way toward reducing the fear and anxiety inherent in that role. The staff should explain procedures, policies, etc., but if they do not, or the explanation has not been understood, the patient or family needs to ask for further or repeated explanation.

In some facilities a family conference is a place and time where explanations happen. Two Mayo Clinic physicians wrote that effective communication is key. Protection of patient autonomy and the honoring of a patient's wishes hinge on a family conference where full disclosure of the patient's condition is communicated by the attending physician and is presented "unambiguously, honestly, and with deep compassion."[20]

Informed consent/informed refusal. Truly, this is a part of explanation, but I separate it because of its importance. Suffice it to say, every procedure needs to be explained in full, with risks and goals of said procedure clearly communicated. Informed consent is more than a piece of paper, and patients need to be clear in their understanding of what is being proposed. Ask questions for any needed clarification.

An important term here is capacity. Capacity is presumed, unless shown otherwise: adults have the ability to decide for themselves and can participate in informed consent. If the adult loses capacity, a surrogate is to make choices based on the patient's values.

Informed refusal. The patient and/or surrogate need to understand clearly what is being refused and the possible consequences of such refusal.

Pain. This is the hospital or life experience to which no one looks forward. What can be done to help? Patients are now routinely asked about pain, to try to quantify any pain they have. Patients are asked to rate their pain along a scale of 0–10, with 0 being no pain and 10 being the worst pain of someone's life. As may be obvious, the higher the number, the more likely the need for pain medication. For lower numbers other interventions may be sufficient.

Positional changes. The nursing staff spends a good amount of time trying to help patients be comfortably situated in their bed or chair. This can help prevent pain and also relieve it at times.

Medication. Analgesia, the relief of pain without loss of consciousness, is the aim. That may be accomplished through oral medications, skin patches, or intravenous drips. Doctors—and patients—have many choices for pain control. Narcotics given intravenously (by IV) may be given by the nursing staff or may be delivered through a specially designed pump the patient can administer (within preset limitations, of course).

---

[20] Eelco Wijdicks, MD, and Alejandro Rabinstein, MD, "End-of-Life Guidelines at Work for Comatose Patients," *Neurology* 68, no. 14 (2007): 1,097–2,000, 1092–94, accessed May 29, 2013, http://www.neurology.org/content/68/14/1092.extract.

Each medication, though, from acetaminophen or nonsteroidal anti-inflammatory drugs (NSAIDs) to oxycodone or morphine, has potential side effects that limit dosage or ability to tolerate the drug. Gastrointestinal (GI) irritation or bleeding can be a problem with certain medications. Some affect the liver; others, the kidneys, but that is not all. Narcotic pain medications are notorious for their effects on the bowel, causing constipation. Bed rest and narcotics are a powerful combination in this regard in that they both slow down the gut.

Pain control may be helped with the addition of medications that enhance the effects of the pain medication. Consultation with a pain specialist, usually a neurologist specially trained in pain management, a palliative care physician, or hospice staff can help in cases where the pain is particularly severe.

CBM: So we are back to pain management. The problem of pain has been one of the major arguments for the pro-euthanasia movement. The argument, put crudely, is, if we can euthanize our animals when they are in pain and are suffering, why not allow euthanizing Granny?

Before we discuss the movement, it is important to get clarity on terminology.

Physician-assisted suicide is the practice of the physician providing the means for the patient to kill himself or herself. For instance, a physician might prescribe a lethal dose of a medication and instruct the patient how much to take in order to die.

Euthanasia, on the other hand, is where the physician actually administers the lethal drug to the patient. In the first instance the patient is the direct agent, and in the second the physician is the direct agent.

Euthanasia can take several forms. First, in *voluntary active euthanasia*, the patient requests a lethal drug the physician actively administers directly. In *nonvoluntary euthanasia* the patient does not request to die, but the physician takes it upon himself to administer a lethal dose of a drug. *Involuntary euthanasia* involves a physician killing a patient medically *against* the patient's wishes. *Passive euthanasia* is a term hardly used any longer. It refers to the removal of life-sustaining treatments like breathing machines and technologically or "artificially" administered nutrition and hydration.

Because most people recognize that a time can come for removing technology, with proper consent, so the dying process can proceed, "euthanasia" seems to be an inappropriate way to describe the act. Withholding and withdrawal of treatment has become a separate category in ethics discussion. Those distinctions become important when discussing the law and policy around the world.

As a physician, help us think about what the legalization of physician-assisted suicide and euthanasia might mean for medicine.

DJR: Our family recently learned a bit about euthanasia for animals. Our beloved dog, Biff, had to be euthanized. Biff was a cockapoo (with a few other breeds thrown in for good measure) and had been the canine member of our household for fourteen years. He had a wonderful disposition and was a great family dog. Eight years ago an endocrine tumor was diagnosed, and within the past year he began showing its effects. He drank large amounts of water and had to be taken outside more and more often. He suffered from some arthritis, which made climbing the steps difficult. His liver became so enlarged that he sometimes dragged his abdomen on the steps outside and inside our home. He fell often and ran into things in the dark due to cataracts that were blinding him. He ceased to bark at the doorbell because he had lost his hearing. When he needed to be taken out every forty-five minutes during the day, we concluded that we could not continue this regimen. Converting him to an outside dog was not an answer for a variety of reasons. His veterinarian was wonderful, and he walked us through the process. We took Biff to the vet, placed him on the table, told him what a wonderful dog he had been to our family, and then held him as the vet gave him the lethal injection. Biff looked momentarily relieved. Then, mercifully, he died.

Several countries around the world have legalized physician-assisted suicide and euthanasia, the Netherlands being the first and most prominent example. The Royal Dutch Medical Association published guidelines for voluntary, active, euthanasia (VAE) only months before the Dutch Supreme Court's 1984 decision to allow physicians to carry out VAE in certain circumstances of "necessity." In *Euthanasia, Ethics and Public Policy*, Georgetown ethicist and law professor John Keown describes the defense of "necessity" this way:

This defence operates to justify . . . the actions of a person who has broken the law, but who has acted responsibly and proportionately in doing so to secure a higher value recognised by the law. A simple example would be the action of pulling a jaywalker from the path of an oncoming car. The law, upholding the values of human autonomy and bodily integrity, generally prohibits touching others without their consent. But it condones the action of one who pulls a jaywalker to safety even though there is no time to seek his consent.[21]

What has happened in the Netherlands? Keown analyzes the results of two large surveys done there and concludes,

1. VAE, certainly not rare, is increasingly performed.
2. Most cases of VAE have been "unreported and unchecked."[22]
3. Guidelines for VAE have been "ignored in practice" and "diluted in theory."[23]

A hospice physician in Holland concluded: "Almost seventy percent of physicians in the Netherlands have been involved in euthanasia of some sort. Yet there is virtually no training in treating dying patients and coping with the impending death. None of the medical schools offer any thorough training for their young students. It is unbelievable how we deny the importance of such training."[24]

In the United States, Oregon was the first state to allow physician-assisted suicide (PAS) where, at the request of a patient (certain parameters being met), a physician can prescribe a lethal dose of barbiturates. The patient takes the medicine whenever he or she wishes to do so. A comparison of the data from 1998, the year of inception in Oregon, and 2010 follows:

---

[21] John Keown, *Euthanasia, Ethics and Public Policy* (Cambridge: Cambridge University Press, 2002), 83.

[22] Ibid., 147.

[23] Ibid., 148.

[24] Zbigniew Zylic, "Palliative Care: Dutch Hospices and Euthanasia," in *Asking to Die*, ed. David C. Thomasma et al. (1998), 198–99, cited in Keown, *Euthanasia, Ethics and Public Policy*, 140–41.

	1998	**2010**
Patients referred for counseling	4	1
PAS prescriptions written	24*	96
Physicians prescribing lethal meds	14	59
Deaths from PAS	16*	65

*Numbers amended from 23 and 15, respectively, in subsequent reports.

Over the dozen intervening years in Oregon, the numbers tell a dark tale: more doctors are writing more prescriptions, and more people are dying through PAS, which some Oregonians call "death with dignity." Every index, *except referrals for counseling*, has increased. Though the numbers may be relatively small, each represents numerous lives affected, for neither the patients nor the physicians live in a vacuum. Ideas have consequences, and so do actions.

Physician Kenneth R. Stevens, a radiation oncologist, pointed to some damning evidence from the report in a Guest Commentary on *Oregon.com*:

> The report did reveal, however, that two patients who attempted to take the supposedly lethal drugs did not die. The report's sparse information states that one person regained consciousness within 24 hours and died of the underlying illness five days later, a second person regained consciousness three days after ingestion of the drugs and died of the underlying illness three months later.[25]

Dr. Stevens wonders in print why these two individuals did not choose to repeat the dose of "lethal medication." He finds it "strange to live in a society where a failed suicide is considered to be unsuccessful and an accomplished suicide is considered a success."[26]

Oregon is not the only state where such changes have come to pass. Washington, Montana, and now Vermont have jumped on

---

[25] Kenneth R. Stevens, "Doctor-assisted suicide: Annual report raises more questions than answers," *OregonLive.com*, February 11, 2011, http://www.oregonlive.com/opinion/index.ssf/2011/02/doctor-ssisted_suicide_annual.html.
[26] Ibid.

the PAS bandwagon. Others have entertained pro-PAS legislation but have not yet joined the ranks of these states.

When John Keown evaluated the 1984 Dutch decision, he raised some poignant questions germane to this discussion. The "necessity defense" had previously been used to save lives; now it is being used to take them. Thus, the court turned this provision of the law on its head. Keown also noted that the judgment "failed to explain *why* the doctor's duty to alleviate suffering overrode his duty not to kill." The notion that one is to relieve suffering by relieving the sufferer of life is perverse logic indeed. Finally, asks Keown, "What qualifies *doctors* to decide when it is right to kill patients?"[27]

Advocating for assisted suicide, Timothy E. Quill, MD, published an account of his patient's death in the venerable *New England Journal of Medicine*.[28] The "Sounding Board" section, a regular feature of the journal, included a slightly longer version. The following is my synopsis of the story.

Diane's rash and fatigue had a dreaded name: acute myelomonocytic leukemia, a particularly virulent form of leukemia, the aggressive treatment of which at that time resulted in a 25 percent long-term cure rate. The cost of treatment is prohibitive not only in terms of dollars and cents but also in the toll it exacts from the bearer. Diane, a survivor of familial (including her own) alcoholism, as well as a bout of vaginal cancer, decided not to pursue treatment. She opted instead for time with her husband, son, and friends, all colored by the fact that her life would soon be over. She saw two hematologist-oncologists and a psychologist she had seen previously and did not change her mind regarding her plan of action. As she worsened and the time of her death approached, she was fearful of a protracted and uncomfortable death. Dr. Quill understood that Diane wanted to control her death and referred her to the Hemlock Society. She later requested from Dr. Quill barbiturates for sleeplessness. He complied and "made sure that she knew how to use the barbiturates for sleep, and also that she knew the amount needed to commit suicide."[29] Some time later Diane

[27] Keown, *Euthanasia, Ethics and Public Policy*, 85.

[28] Timothy E. Quill, "Death and Dignity, A Case of Individualized Decision Making," *New England Journal of Medicine* 324, no. 10 (March 7, 1991): 691–94.

[29] Ibid., 693.

asked her husband and son to leave her for an hour, and when they
returned, she was dead. Dr. Quill informed the medical examiner
of the death of a hospice patient and gave as the cause of death,
"acute leukemia." Dr. Quill explained his reasoning:

> So I said "acute leukemia" to protect all of us, to protect
> Diane from an invasion into her past and her body, and
> to continue to shield society from the knowledge of the
> degree of suffering that people often undergo in the pro-
> cess of dying. Suffering can be lessened to some extent,
> but in no way eliminated or made benign, by the careful
> intervention of a competent, caring physician, given cur-
> rent social constraints.[30]

This description is remarkable for several reasons. First, it is
a public admission in an influential medical journal of a physician who has been party, albeit indirectly, to a suicide. Second,
the tone of the piece is entirely sympathetic to physician-assisted
suicide and exalts patient autonomy as the most valuable of medical goods. Third, the author admits not telling the whole truth
to the medical examiner. Finally, he is frustrated that physicians
are limited to something he considers less than the elimination
of suffering.[31] He is also influencing physicians and future physicians: this article is required reading for medical students in a
number of medical schools, offered as a portion of their medical ethics training. Further, the article is discussed in what has
become the Bible of bioethics, *Principles of Biomedical Ethics* by
Beauchamp and Childress. The authors summarize this case and
comment:

> Despite these problems, we do not oppose Quill's act, his
> patient's decision, or their relationship. Suffering and loss
> of cognitive capacity can ravage and dehumanize patients
> so severely that death is in their best interests. In these
> tragic situations—or in anticipation of them, as in this
> case—physicians like Quill do not act wrongly in assisting
> competent patients, at their request, to bring about their

[30] Ibid., 694.
[31] Ibid.

deaths. Public policy issues regarding how to avoid abuses and discourage unjustified acts should be a central part of our discussion about forms of appropriate physician assistance, but these issues do not affect the moral justifiability of the physician's act itself.

We maintain that physician assistance in hastening death is best viewed as part of a continuum of medical care.[32]

What happens when physicians, long trained as healers, become purveyors of poisons (in the Hippocratic sense and in truth)? The Netherlands, Oregon, and the endorsement of Dr. Quill by the medical ethics establishment give us a clue. The number of physicians participating initially would be small but would increase over time. The number of patients receiving prescriptions and taking the medications would also increase over time. At first the participation would be voluntary. "If you don't want to die, don't drink the poison" would be the axiom. Eventually definitions would be enlarged. If assisted suicide becomes a "right," then a patient cannot be denied that right just because he or she is unable to request or administer it. Others would need to be enlisted to "decide in the patient's best interests" and "help the patient do what he or she cannot do." And why should we require assisted death to be voluntary? If a patient has not expressed his wishes, the argument would run, but if it is in his interests to be euthanized, we need not get his permission, especially if he is unable to communicate because of a coma. Already some elderly patients in Holland are fearful they will be euthanized without their consent.[33] In comments to Britain's House of Lords, Lord McColl referenced the Dutch Patients' Association, 6,000 members of which carry cards stating that they do not want euthanasia if they are taken into hospital or a nursing home.[34] Should we be surprised?

[32] Tom L. Beauchamp and James F. Childress, *Principles of Biomedical Ethics* (New York: Oxford University Press, 2009), 183–84.

[33] See Carlos F. Gomez, *Regulating Death: Euthanasia and the Case of the Netherlands* (New York: Free Press, 1991).

[34] Martin Beckford, "Fearful Elderly People Carry 'Anti-euthanasia Cards'," *The Telegraph*, April 21, 2011, accessed February 3, 2014, http://www.telegraph.co.uk/health/healthnews/8466996/Fearful-elderly-people-carry-anti-euthanasia-cards.html.

Perhaps a thought experiment would help us see the effects of healers turned killers. Consider that the chefs of a particular city are given permission to poison people who request it. The license, hanging on the wall for all the patrons to see, does not differ between those who poison upon request and those who do not. Now consider that you take your family to a restaurant in that city. You are seated by the hostess like everyone else. A pleasant-appearing older couple is seated at the next table, enjoying their meal. You scan the menu, and it looks good. You order your food and occupy yourself with taking in the view while you wait for the server to bring your dinner. The older gentleman at the next table appears to be falling asleep at his meal. How comfortable would you feel as you pick up your fork to taste your salad? What assurance would you have that you would not be next?

Euthanizing our dog was difficult. The expert, the vet with the needle, assured us that it was the right thing to do and the right time to do it. We ultimately agreed, and the irreversible deed was done. We had tried to prepare our sons for the event over the previous few months, as the dog was becoming increasingly decrepit. The only son in town at the time came over the night before the event to say good-bye to his furry friend. Others were away so we decided to have Biff cremated in order for them to be able to bid him adieu when they returned. Even with all that preparation, it was a difficult event. Tears flowed, and the routines of feeding and walking were strangely absent. I know and accept that I was primarily responsible for the timing of the death of our dog. I simply was worn out with caring for him. Under the bright light of scrutiny, however, his death was a convenience for me. That, after all, is what euthanasia turns out to be: a convenience.

Dying well is hard work. Helping others, as they die, to die well can be equally hard work.

CBM: Dying well. That puts us deep in theological territory. The church has had much to say about dying well and faithfully. In a magnificent book by Duke Divinity School professor Allen Verhey, *The Christian Art of Dying: Learning from Jesus*, the author offers what he calls a contemporary *Ars Moriendi*. Dating back to the Middle Ages, the *Ars Moriendi* ("The Art of Dying") was composed of two books written against the backdrop of the horrors of the

Black Death (c. 1350), a bacterial plague that killed 30–60 percent of Europe's population. The *Ars Moriendi* contained instructions for how to prepare well for death. "Today the title would probably be something like *Dying Well for Dummies*," quips Verhey.[35]

Verhey celebrates the powers of contemporary medicine and its ability to preserve life, but he worries about the "medicalization of death." At least since Francis Bacon, the West has been a champion of the improvement of life through the advancement of science. Bacon was suspicious of the notion that someone must be "overmastered by their disease." Science should come to the rescue. Physicians should be the proper soldiers in this battle. "Their courage was their refusal to call any disease incurable. Their weapons were forged in scientific study and research. Their allies were the universities and its laboratories."[36]

So today, at the other end of the Baconian project, we are in pursuit of a technologically achieved immortality. Until that is realized, however, we relegate dying, especially in its finality, death, to hospitals. Why? Well, among other reasons, hospitals are our "magazines," the places we store our weapons against death.

Verhey begins his defense of a contemporary *Ars Moriendi* by commending life: "Life is a gift of God, a gift of the God who gives humans breath and calls them to get a heart of wisdom."[37] From the biblical perspective, death is an enemy.

> In the context of the recognition of mortality, some deaths may be regarded as better than others, but none are regarded as good. A bad death was a premature death, a death, as Hezekiah said, "in the noontide of my days" (Isa. 38:10). A bad death was a death by violence, death "by the sword" (e.g., Amos 7:11). A bad death was a death without an heir (e.g., Ecclesiasticus 44:9). In the death of Absalom all three features of a bad death come together; he died young, violently, and without an heir (2 Sam. 18). In comparison, other deaths are not so bad: death "in a good old age" and "in peace" (as God promised to Abraham, Gen. 15:15),

---

[35] Allen Verhey, *The Christian Art of Dying: Learning from Jesus* (Grand Rapids, MI: Eerdmans, 2010), 79.

[36] Ibid., 31.

[37] Ibid., 180.

death surrounded by one's children (as Jacob in Balaam's praise, Num. 23:10). Such deaths are better by far, but they are not therefore good. The bad death is particularly to be lamented, but no death is simply celebrated.[38]

The *Ars Moriendi* tradition, Verhey explains, points to Jesus as the model for a Christian's faithful dying. "Let the dying remember Jesus and think about the passion of Christ."[39] Nevertheless, Jesus's death is *sui generis*, one of a kind, and is not easily applied to our situations in a practical sense. Despite that caution, Jesus' faithfulness, hope, patience, love, humility, and courage are worthy of imitation.

Verhey maintains that the first of the virtues for dying well and faithfully is faith. "Dying reminds us that we are radically dependent creatures. It reminds us that our existence is contingent and that we are not in control of our own existing."[40] Just as Jesus trusted his Father, we must trust God in dying. He did not respond to dying by asserting his own prerogatives or by denying the awful reality of his own death, but, as the psalmist prayed, "Father, into Your hands I entrust My spirit" (Ps 31:5; Luke 23:46).

> To die well, no less than to live well, you have to care about life, but you also have to care about some things more than you care about survival. Self-absorbed anxiety is the enemy of faithfulness unto death. And this egocentric anxiety may include the anxiety about whether our souls will go to heaven when we die. The remedy for that anxiety is not to make a last-ditch effort to appease God with the right words or right works, as if either the little truth we know well or the little good we do well could provide a ticket to heaven. The remedy is not faith in faith but faith in God. The remedy is to trust the God who created the world and promises to make it new.[41]

Hope—the confidence that God is, and ever will be, faithful—follows from faith. Death threatens to undo us, to brutalize us, to kill us. Through the resurrection of Christ, God has given

---

[38] Ibid.
[39] Ibid., 216.
[40] Ibid., 257.
[41] Ibid., 260–61.

us grounds to hope that death, however awful, will not have the last word. Because Jesus has been raised from the dead, the Holy Spirit has been poured out as the firstfruits and guarantee of a good future with God (Rom 8:23; Eph 1:13). God has won the victory over death, inspiring hope.

> Christians hope because they know the faithfulness of the One who made all things, because they know the story of one who was raised from the dead, and because they know a life-giving Spirit. The Christian church owns a story in canon and creed that begins with the power and love of the Creator, centers in the resurrection of the crucified Jesus, and ends with talk of God's good future—and our own. They cannot but hope.[42]

The virtue of love, according to Verhey, is not to be equated with desire, or even care *per se*. "Love is fundamentally an affective affirmation of the other."[43] The "other" in this case is, of course, both God and neighbor. We love God because he first loved us. Gratitude flows from love of God. Yet, "[t]here is no loving God that does not also love the neighbor (1 John 4:20; see also 3:17; 4:12)."[44] This love evokes a readiness to reconcile and be reconciled, to forgive and be forgiven. "We do not die well or faithfully," counsels Verhey, "by carrying a grudge to our graves."[45] This is why, historically speaking, a sudden death was not desirable. It would give no opportunity to make things right with loved ones and friends.

Affective affirmation of the other manifests itself in wanting to be with those we love. Hardly anything can be more horrible than dying alone and hardly anything more comforting than dying surrounded by those we love and who love us. One of the tragic consequences of the medicalization of dying and death is the separation from loved ones that often occurs.

Patience is another important virtue for facing dying—not Stoic resignation but persevering dependence on the goodness of God. "Christian patience acknowledges and affirms that we are

---

[42] Ibid., 145.
[43] Ibid.
[44] Ibid.
[45] Ibid., 277.

dependent creatures," writes Verhey. "It trains us to receive care
graciously and gratefully. It trains us to accept both the dependency of others and our own dependency."[46] Unlike Stoic *apatheia*,
Christian patience does not celebrate suffering. "But patience is
ready to endure and to share suffering for the sake of love."[47] The
Stoic answer to suffering included the option to end one's own life.
"Christian patience, however, makes no place for suicide."[48] In fact,
early theologians were consistent in their insistence that suicide was
sub-Christian at best because hope and love sustain patience.

Humility is contrasted with self-righteousness and autonomy in
Verhey's account of the virtues. Pride gets in the way of dying well
and faithfully since it claims self-sufficiency. Yet few of life's experiences reveal our dependence and fragility more than dying.

> The temptation of pride comes long before the death-
> bed, of course, but when we are dying, the habit of pride
> makes dying well difficult. It can make those in need of
> care ashamed of "being a burden" and resentful of those
> compassionate caregivers whose very care reminds us of
> just how needy we are.
>
> Such pride is folly, of course. None of us is as autono-
> mous and independent as we like to claim. I have been a
> burden to those I love—and to those who love me—for
> quite a while now. I started as a baby, as all of us do, and I
> remain dependent on others, as all of us also do, whether
> we acknowledge it or not.[49]

The final virtue Verhey elucidates is difficult to name, so he calls
it letting go/serenity/generosity. Its opposite is the tightfisted grip
of anxiety one feels when one holds too tightly to life. Today, rather
than cultivate this virtue, we appeal to psychopharmaceuticals—
drugs—to dull the anxiety. In doing so, we disable our ability to
attend to the meaning of life, death, and suffering. This does not
argue, says Verhey, that it is inappropriate to offer palliatives, but it
is wrong to see palliation as a cure. The ultimate antidote to anxiety
is to look to Jesus, the one who commands us not to be anxious

---

[46] Ibid., 279.
[47] Ibid., 280.
[48] Ibid.
[49] Ibid., 286.

(Matt 6:31; Luke 12:22) because God is faithful, he cares for us, and he has secured the future.

> Surely our anxiety and pride are related to our avarice, to the anxious tightfistedness that is unwilling to let go of the things we think will establish our independence and security against need. Death will leave us empty-handed, but on the way to death we will die well and faithfully if we learn to open our hands, to open them humbly and thankfully toward the blessing of God and to open them gratefully and generously toward others in love. In both cases we open them toward the good future of God.[50]

Finally, courage is required to die well and faithfully. We do not commend death. It is an enemy. Courage enables us to face the enemy without fear because it is underwritten by faith, hope, love, humility, and serenity. Because of Jesus, we can face dying and death with confidence.

Increasingly throughout the Old Testament witness, emphasis was placed on the hope of the bodily resurrection. "Whether the resurrection of the body could be 'proved from Torah' or not, it was 'an intelligible development of the faith contained in the Hebrew Scriptures.' Jewish confidence in God was bound by its own integrity to move in the direction of such a hope."[51] Moreover, bodily resurrection was much more consistent with Old Testament anthropology than the dualism of the Platonic tradition.

Jesus fulfilled Israel's expectation that through Messiah God would defeat the power of sin and death, establishing his sovereignty over the entire created order. They believed resurrection would come at the end of time. Yet, because no one was anticipating a resurrection "in the middle of time," Jesus' resurrection was unintelligible to many Jewish people of his day. For others the resurrection of Jesus was indeed that long-hoped-for apocalyptic event with eschatological implications.

The resurrection—a divine victory, not a technological victory—guarantees that we will not be alienated from our flesh, our community, or from God's good future. Nothing can separate us from the love of God. Not even death; especially not death.

---

[50] Ibid.
[51] Ibid., 190.

Conclusion

Dying well, for most of us, will mean preparing ourselves for dying. Unless we leave this life suddenly, we will have some time to prepare. Contrary to our culture of flippancy about most things, reflecting on one's dying is neither morbid nor a sign of maladjustment. It has only been in the latter part of the twentieth century that individuals have had the luxury of *not* thinking about death and dying.

How should we prepare ourselves for dying?

- Live well. For the Christian, living well means bringing glory to God by becoming more like Jesus. Growing in Christlikeness in every area of life is the best way to prepare for dying.
- Keep household and business affairs in order. Organizing important documents—including advance directives—can be a gift to one's family. Getting together one's will and testament, bank documents, etc., can help remove the fear of dying suddenly.
- Make a bucket list. Life is short. There is nothing wrong with aspiring to do or see new things before it ends.
- Keep short accounts with God and others. Bitterness, anger, malice, and envy can destroy one's joy. Don't let them build up. Reconcile with spouses, family, and others.
- Prearrange the funeral. Doing so not only relieves family members of the burden during a time when they are emotionally wrought, but it ensures the arrangements will be consistent with your wishes.

Additional Resources

Byock, Ira. *Dying Well: Peace and Possiblities at the End of Life*. New York: Riverhead, 1998.

Cameron, Nigel M. de S., ed. *Death Without Dignity: Euthanasia in Perspective*. Edinburgh: Rutherford House, 1990.

Dunlop, John. *Finishing Well to the Glory of God: Strategies from a Christian Physician*. Wheaton, IL: Crossway, 2011.

Moll, Rob. *The Art of Dying: Living Fully into the Life to Come*. Downers Grove, IL: InterVarsity, 2010.

Smith, Wesley J. *Culture of Death: The Assault on Medical Ethics in America*. New York: Encounter, 2000.

Part III

Making Life

Chapter 5

Infertility and Assisted Reproductive Technologies

Case: The Surrogate Pianist

J
ane, a twenty-five-year-old single female, has been playing the piano at First Church for two years. She is paid by the church and is viewed not only as a part-time employee but as part of the ministry team at the church. A near life-time member of First Church, Jane's father is a deacon and his family well respected in the community.

For several weeks Dr. I. M. Pious, the senior pastor, noticed that Jane was putting on weight. Not one to ask impertinent questions, Pastor Pious kept his observations between himself and his wife until it was obvious that Jane was showing signs of pregnancy.

At a Monday morning staff meeting, Pastor Pious asked the other members of the pastoral staff if they knew Jane's status. No one knew anything informative about Jane's life, but all agreed she was definitely pregnant. Eventually they decided that someone should talk to her.

After the next Sunday morning worship service, Pastor Pious and music minister H. M. Singer invited Jane to meet in the pastor's study for a few moments. They exchanged pleasantries, and the pastor then broached the question of Jane's obvious pregnancy.

"Yes, Pastor, I am pregnant," she responded. Then, without blushing, Jane said, "But, Pastor, don't worry. I'm still a virgin."

Since First Church is an evangelical church, the pastors affirmed the reality of the virgin birth, but they believed it was a one-time event!

Upon further discussion the pastors learned that Jane's married elder sister, Eileen, and her husband, Phil, had been trying unsuccessfully to get pregnant for over two years. Twice Eileen had miscarried because of a uterine condition that made it impossible for her to carry a baby to term. She and Phil were devastated after the last miscarriage and vowed they could not go through that again.

Hearing their plight, the fertility specialist told them they could be excellent candidates for a surrogacy arrangement. All they needed was to locate a healthy woman who could carry their baby to term. Using in vitro fertilization, Phil and Eileen's embryos could be transferred to the surrogate, and she could gestate the baby until birth. The specialist informed the couple that they could either employ a surrogate for money (as a "commercial" surrogate), or they might be able to find a friend or family member who would volunteer (an "altruistic" surrogate). That's when the couple thought about asking Jane if she would be willing to carry their baby.

When Eileen and Phil approached Jane, she was immediately enthusiastic about the invitation to be a surrogate mother. Theirs was a close-knit family, and as the baby's aunt, she would help rear the child anyway. She was more than willing to offer her uterus to her sister and brother-in-law. It seemed to be the least she could do for them. And because fertilization would take place technologically, she could continue to preserve her virginity. She is now six months pregnant.

Questions for Reflection

1. Would it make a difference in the case if Jane was a commercial surrogate instead of an altruistic surrogate?

2. Why didn't Jane seek the counsel of her pastors *before* she made the decision to become a surrogate?

3. What responsibility do Phil and Eileen bear in the decision?

4. Should Jane be asked to step down from playing the piano while she is pregnant?

5. What biblical norms or principles ought to be considered before reaching a decision in this case?

Discussion

C. Ben Mitchell (CBM): When I first entered pastoral ministry, most of the medical ethical questions I encountered involved the end of life. A family would ask me, "The doctors say it's time to remove the ventilator. What should we do?" Questions arose like: Is brain death really death? Should we maintain tube feeding and hydration? Those are still important questions. But today ethical questions are just as likely to arise around the beginning of life. Increasingly, it seems, couples are grappling with infertility and trying to navigate the alphabet soup of technologies that promise to provide them with a baby. How did we get where we are now?

D. Joy Riley (DJR): Let's start with what some have called the "Reproductive Revolution." Arguably that revolution began with the birth of Louise Joy Brown, the world's first "test-tube baby" on July 25, 1978. Embryologist Robert Edwards partnered with obstetrician/gynecologist Patrick Steptoe in developing the technique called in vitro fertilization (IVF). *In vitro*, literally "in glass," indicates where the fertilization actually takes place. Edwards was awarded a Nobel Prize for his work in reproductive technology in 2010.

Louise Brown reacted to the Nobel announcement: "It's fantastic news—me and mum are so glad that one of the pioneers of IVF has been given the recognition he deserves."[1] One might ask why the three decades' wait to award Edwards a Nobel for his work. After all, by 2010, approximately 4 million children had been born

---

[1] "Creator of IVF Robert Edwards Awarded Nobel Prize for Medicine," *Herald Sun*, October 5, 2010, accessed March 30, 2012, http://www.heraldsun.com.au/news/more-news/creator-of-ivf-robert-edwards-awarded-nobel-prize-for-medicine/story-e6frf7lf-1225934126176.

through IVF worldwide. According to the jury, "Long-term follow-up studies have shown that IVF children are as healthy as other children."[2] The health concern of the medical and scientific communities regarding the subsequent generation played a role. Were there other concerns?

Despite its apparent success, IVF has not been endorsed by everyone. The Catholic Church found the procedure problematic from the beginning. In an interview Robert Edwards gave on the twenty-fifth anniversary of Louise Brown's birth, he revealed his thoughts about the church's reprimand:

> The Vatican called Louise's birth "an event that can have very grave consequences for humanity" because it divorced the conjugal sexual act from procreation. . . .
>
> "It was a fantastic achievement but it was about more than infertility," says Edwards, who rarely gives interviews but, when he does, delights in speaking his mind. "It was also about issues like stem cells and the ethics of human conception. I wanted to find out exactly who was in charge, whether it was God Himself or whether it was scientists in the laboratory."
>
> And what did he conclude? "It was us," he smiles triumphantly. "The Pope looked totally stupid. You can never ban anything. You can say, hang on a minute. But never say never, and never say that this is the worst decision for humankind, otherwise you can look a fool. Now there are as many Roman Catholics coming for treatment as Protestants."[3]

Louise Joy Brown and her sister, along with millions of others born through IVF, display the happy side of assisted reproductive technologies (ART), though not every story ends so happily. The issues surrounding ART are increasingly complex and need sorting out.

CBM: Before we reflect on those technologies and try to get to grips with the ethics of ART, could you give us a brief biology

---

[2] Ibid.
[3] Anjana Ahuja, "'God Is Not in Charge, We Are,'" *The Times*, July 24, 2003, accessed March 30, 2012, http://www.thetimes.co.uk/tto/life/article1716703.ece (subscription required).

refresher course? We want to be sure we get the science and the terminology right.

Back to Basics

DJR: Though this may seem somewhat technical, for couples to make informed decisions about reproductive technologies, they will need to become familiar with some basic medical facts. I should also mention here that I am not an Ob/Gyn (although I am married to one) and, especially, not an infertility specialist. I have studied the subject for several years both as a physician and as an interested commentator.

Most of the cells in a human body contain a nucleus. Normal nuclei of cells contain forty-six chromosomes, which carry genetic information, or genes. The exception is a gamete (a reproductive cell)—either sperm or egg. Each gamete has only twenty-three, or half of the full complement of human chromosomes. When a sperm fertilizes an egg, the two sets of twenty-three chromosomes combine to form the forty-six chromosomes of a brand-new, genetically unique, human being.

At birth baby girls carry about two million egg cells, or oocytes, but this decreases to about 400,000 by the onset of puberty. Although a woman only ovulates one or two eggs per menstrual cycle, she loses about a thousand premature oocytes per month until age thirty-five years, when the rate of loss increases. Over her reproductive lifetime, she ovulates approximately 400 egg cells.[4] It was previously thought that all the egg cells she can ever have are present at birth, but the recent discovery of egg stem cells has challenged that perception.

On the male side things are different. Sperm are not produced until the testosterone level increases at puberty. Multiple divisions of cells eventually become sperm. In fact, the entire cycle of sperm production, or spermatogenesis, takes seventy-four days. The testis contains multiple generations, however, so that daily sperm production numbers in the millions in fertile males. There are age-related changes in sperm production. The seminiferous tubules of the testis, where sperm are ultimately produced, tell a story that

---

[4] Karen D. Bradshaw, "The Ovary and the Menstrual Cycle," in *Precis: An Update in Obstetrics and Gynecology—Reproductive Endocrinology*, 3rd ed. (Washington, DC: The American College of Obstetricians and Gynecologists, 2007), 56.

is not completely understood. In men ages twenty-seven to forty-two, about 85 percent of the seminiferous tubules show normal spermatogenesis. Those numbers decrease to ~31 percent in men ages seventy to seventy-nine and ~16 percent in men eighty to eighty-nine years of age.[5]

An ejaculate of semen—sperm with attendant fluid—usually measures 1.5–5.0 milliliters and contains 70–80 million sperm per milliliter in fertile populations. Studies of sperm placed in the vagina resulted in only one in 5,000 sperm reaching the cervical mucus, and one in 14 million sperm reaching the oviduct, or fallopian tube, where normal fertilization occurs.[6] Life is, indeed, a miracle!

The anatomy of the normal human female reproductive tract is shown below.

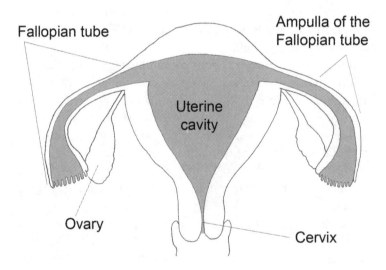

Normal Female Reproductive Tract Schematic © D. Joy Riley, 2013

---

[5] Patrick C. Walsh, Alan B. Retik, E. Darracott Vaughan Jr., and Alan J. Wein, eds., *Campbell's Urology*, 7th ed., vol. 2 (Philadelphia: W. B. Saunders, 1998), 1,263–68.
[6] Ibid., 1,290–96.

The uterus opens to the interior of the pelvis through two Fallopian tubes and to the vagina through the cervix. The Fallopian tubes have fringed ends that resemble fingers in the diagram. Approximately once a month during a woman's reproductive years, a mature egg (or two, occasionally) is released from an ovary. This is ovulation. The egg is taken into the Fallopian tube and journeys from there into the uterus. During sexual intercourse sperm are ejaculated and travel upward through the vagina, cervix, uterus, and out into the Fallopian tubes in the opposite direction and toward the released egg(s). Fertilization—the penetration of the sperm into the egg with the combination of their genomes—typically occurs in the ampulla of the Fallopian tube. Whether or not the egg is fertilized, it continues its journey through the tube and into the uterus. If the egg is fertilized, a pregnancy results, and normally the embryo implants into the uterine lining. If the egg is not fertilized, it is expelled along with the innermost lining cells of the uterus; this is a period, otherwise known as "menses."

CBM: That is extremely helpful. Knowing that pregnancy occurs at fertilization rather than at implantation will help us make several important distinctions later. Having this basic understanding of human reproduction helps us understand infertility. When a couple says their doctor has given them a diagnosis of infertility, what does that mean?

DJR: *Infertility* is defined as "the inability to conceive after twelve months of regular, unprotected heterosexual intercourse." According to standard medical texts, this definition is based on "expected monthly conception rates of 20–25% among healthy young couples and studies demonstrating that 85% of normal couples conceive within 1 year. Therefore, in the United States, approximately 15% of couples are infertile."[7]

The causes of infertility, based on medical evaluation of couples experiencing infertility, can be due to factors in the female or male reproductive tracts, or both. In the table below, causes of infertility

---

[7] Marc A. Fritz, William C. Dodson, David Meldrum, and Julia V. Johnson, "Infertility," in *Precis: an Update in Obstetrics and Gynecology—Reproductive Endocrinology*, 140.

in the United States during the first decade of this century are shown in graph form (see page 115).[8]

The data, collected by the Centers for Disease Control and Prevention (CDC), are available through the website of SART, the Society for Assisted Reproductive Technologies. The public reporting of the data typically lags about two years. The 2011 data, released in 2013, reveals a single female factor accounted for 34 percent infertility, and multiple female factors, 11 percent. The "male factor" was implicated in 17 percent of the diagnoses, and combined female and male factors, 11 percent. Of note is the fact that "unknown" factors accounted for 12 percent infertility in 2011.[9]

CBM: From this chart we can conclude that (1) infertility is a result of a variety and, sometimes, even a combination of problems with both the male's and female's normal reproductive function. But it seems also worth noting that (2) in more than one out of ten couples, there is no known reason for the infertility. This is important in counseling couples. Whether or not the cause of infertility is known, or with whom it originates, the "blame game" does not help anyone.

What are some of the ARTs that are now available? How do they work?

Beyond the Basics—ART in the United States

DJR: A significant number of infertile couples choose to use assisted reproductive technologies. ART involves, "All treatments or procedures that involve surgically removing eggs from a woman's ovaries and combining the eggs with sperm to help a woman become pregnant."[10]

IVF, in which the laboratory-fertilized eggs are inserted into the uterus through the vagina, now represents more than 99 percent of ART procedures in the United States.

---

[8] Data set from the Society for Assisted Reproductive Technology (SART), accessed February 8, 2012, https://www.sartcorsonline.com/rptCSR_PublicMultYear.aspx?ClinicPKID=0.

[9] SART CORS, "Clinic Summary Report: All SART Member Clinics," accessed February 4, 2014, https://www.sartcorsonline.com/rptCSR_PublicMultYear.aspx?ClinicPKID=0.

[10] Appendix B: Glossary of Terms, "2009 Assisted Reproductive Technology Success Rates National Summary and Fertility Clinic Reports," Centers for Disease Control and Prevention, 543, accessed March 30, 2012, http://www.cdc.gov/art/ART2009/section1.htm.

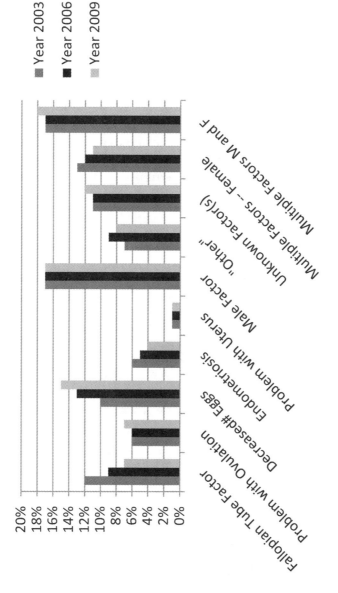

Data set from the Society for Assisted Reproductive Technology (SART) on the causes of infertility, for the years 2003, 2006, and 2009, adapted.

In IVF, a woman is given hormone pills and injections of hormones to cause her to produce multiple eggs. Her eggs, typically a dozen or more, are surgically extracted from the ovary. These ova are placed in a petri dish along with sperm, and fertilization takes place. The fertilized egg—the embryo—is incubated for a few days and then transferred into the woman's uterus, which has been prepared by the hormonal therapy. If the embryo burrows into the lining of the uterus, it is said to "implant."

A common practice now associated with IVF is *intracytoplasmic sperm injection* (ICSI). The process is the same as the one in the diagram except the fertilization step is more controlled. An egg is held in place by vacuum, a small nick is made in the cytoplasmic membrane, and a single sperm (minus a portion of its tail) is injected into the egg. Multiple eggs may be fertilized by this method per

In vitro Fertilization (IVF)

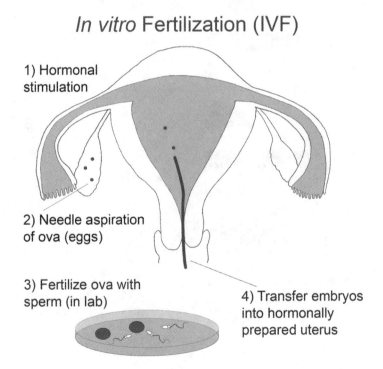

1) Hormonal stimulation

2) Needle aspiration of ova (eggs)

3) Fertilize ova with sperm (in lab)

4) Transfer embryos into hormonally prepared uterus

© D. Joy Riley, 2013

cycle. After incubation one or more embryos are then transferred to the woman's hormonally prepared uterus.

Two other ART procedures that require explanation are:

> *GIFT, gamete intrafallopian transfer.* The eggs are harvested as above, and both sperm and egg are instilled into a Fallopian tube through a second operative procedure. Fertilization, if it takes place, occurs in the Fallopian tube like normal fertilization.

> *ZIFT, zygote intrafallopian transfer.* The eggs are harvested as above and fertilized in the laboratory. The zygote, or embryo, is then transferred into the woman's Fallopian tube through a second surgical procedure.

In 2010, a total of 147,260 ART cycles were reported by 443 clinics in the United States. These resulted in 47,090 live birth deliveries and the birth of 61,564 infants in this country.[11] A multiple birth counts statistically as one live birth, but the individual infants are counted separately. Obviously, then, a substantial number of the births comprised births of twins or higher multiples. According to the CDC, the government agency who tracks the data, "ART accounts for slightly more than 1% of total U.S. births."[12]

CBM: Help us understand what those numbers mean. How successful is IVF?

DJR: Unfortunately, many couples get the impression either from the popular media, from well-meaning friends, or sometimes even from their doctors, that IVF is a miracle cure for their childlessness. The reality is that typically less than one-third of couples undergoing treatment take a baby home as a result of IVF.[13] That number is complicated, for it does not mean each couple's chances of a "successful" IVF cycle are the same. I am not sure how the data will

---

[11] "Where Are United States ART Clinics Located, How Many ART Cycles Did They Perform in 2012, and How Many Infants Were Born from These ART Cycles?," CDC, Section 1: Overview, 2010 ART Report, accessed February 4, 2014, http://www.cdc.gov /art/ART2010/section1.htm.

[12] Ibid.

[13] *2010 Assisted Reproductive Technology Fertility Clinic Success Rates Report,* CDC, American Society for Reproductive Medicine, Society for Assisted Reproductive Technology (Atlanta: US Department of Health and Human Services, 2012), 6, accessed February 4, 2014, http://www.cdc.gov/art/ART2010/PDFs/01_ART_2010_Clinic_Report-FM.pdf.

change if fertile men and women, who are in relationships that are not heterosexual, are added to the "infertile" couples. If the statistics are not separated somehow, the reported rates for "infertile" couples could be artificially inflated. Another contributing factor to "take home baby rates" is the use of sperm or eggs of so-called "donors."

Gamete "Donation"

Gametes—sperm or eggs—are usually exchanged for money in the Unites States, but they are said to be "donated." A man can sell his sperm, but the official title for using it is "donor insemination" (DI). Thus, donor insemination using a husband's sperm is DIH. Donation of a woman's eggs brings a higher price than a man's sperm, but the price reflects the difficulty of the process and the risks involved. Providing semen is much less time-consuming than providing eggs, and it involves no known physical risk. The process of egg "donation," however, usually includes two weeks of daily hormone injections, several ultrasounds and blood draws, and surgical retrieval of the eggs. The risks of extreme discomfort, ovarian hyperstimulation syndrome, and, even though rare, death, are not insignificant. Donor insemination is not, technically speaking, considered an ART, but donor egg cycles are.

The CDC's definition of "donor egg cycle" includes an interesting note: "**Donor egg cycle**. An embryo is formed from the egg of one woman (the donor) and then transferred to another woman who is unable to use her own eggs (the recipient). *The donor relinquishes all parental rights to any resulting offspring*" (emphasis added).[14]

Eggs or embryos were donated in about 12 percent of all ART cycles in the US in 2010.[15] Numbers of pregnancies using donor insemination are not tracked by the CDC.

Donor insemination began in secrecy and collusion, and that legacy permeates donor insemination today. In 1884, the wife of a couple, presenting with infertility due to the husband's lack of sperm, sought help from Dr. William Pancoast of Jefferson

---

[14] CDC, "2009 Assisted Reproductive Technology Success Rates," 543.

[15] "Are Older Women Undergoing ART More Likely to Use Donor Eggs or Embryos?" CDC, Section 4: ART Cycles Using Donor Eggs, accessed February 4, 2014, http://www.cdc.gov/art/ART2010/section4.htm.

Medical College in Philadelphia. A suggestion was made that the most handsome medical student (among six possibilities) supply a sperm sample, which he did. The couple knew nothing of this; indeed, the woman was unconscious. Later the husband alone was informed and did not complain. A son was born from this first documented donor insemination.[16] A survey of the "American sperm industry" by the Office of Technology Assessment in 1987 and 1988 provided an estimate of 30,000 babies born per year from donor insemination (then called AID, artificial insemination by donor).[17]

CBM: That is a long time ago. The fact that donor insemination is not tracked and that the Office of Technology Assessment closed in 1995 contribute to the lack of knowledge about how many births are attributable annually to donor insemination.[18] And that is not all, of course.

DJR: No, that is not all. In his book *The Genius Factory: The Curious History of the Nobel Prize Sperm Bank*, David Plotz traces the "moral arc" of all fertility treatments since donor insemination:

First, Denial: This is physically impossible.
Then Revulsion: This is an outrage against God and nature.
Then Silent Tolerance: You can do it, but please don't talk about it.
Finally, Popular Embrace: Do it, talk about it, brag about it. *You are having test-tube triplets carried by a surrogate? So am I!*[19]

The level of "popular embrace" appears to have been reached with sperm donation. One needs only to consider Trent Arsenault, a sperm donor who has spawned children without sex or responsibility, garnering the title, "The Virgin Father."

---

[16] David Plotz, *The Genius Factory: The Curious History of the Nobel Prize Sperm Bank* (New York: Random House, 2005), 159–60.
[17] Ibid., 170.
[18] "The OTA Legacy," accessed February 4, 2014, http://www.princeton.edu/~ota.
[19] Plotz, *The Genius Factory*, 164.

After he moved to California, he set up a home webcam that streamed 24–7. His parents could log on anytime and see their son. Strangers, too, came across the feed, and he began to receive requests to take off his clothes. Trent was proud of his new body, and he obliged, posting pictures of himself on sites called TrentCats and TrentNude. He was excited by the feedback, and after the launch of Xtube, an amateur porn-sharing platform, he started uploading masturbation videos under the name TrentDog.[20]

This presaged his current activities:

In 2006, Trent hung out a shingle on the Internet and became a do-it-yourself sperm donor, giving his semen away to whoever asked. He was part of a growing movement of peer-to-peer sperm donation that bypassed regulated banks, and in some cases dropped the customary anonymity, but Trent went further, offering unusual transparency by posting records on his website, including STD-test results, his driver's license, family photos, and a link to his Facebook page. . . .
    Since appearing on various television news programs, Trent has received hundreds of encouraging e-mails, and he's closing in on 2,000 Facebook friends.[21]

By the time the article was written, Trent had provided more than 500 free "donations" and fathered fifteen children through fourteen pregnancies.[22]

CBM: It is no wonder that the era of reproductive technologies has been called a revolution. Not only have the past thirty years brought amazing technological developments, but they have also ushered in perplexing, and sometimes frightening, social developments. Christians have lots of work to do in navigating the contours of the culture.
    But let's get back to infertility. How pervasive is it? Just how many couples are affected?

---

[20] Benjamin Wallace, "The Virgin Father," *New York Magazine*, February 5, 2012, accessed April 2, 2012, http://nymag.com/news/features/trent-arsenault-2012-2.
[21] Ibid.
[22] Ibid.

DJR: Infertility often is a traumatic experience for couples, but the numbers are not easily discerned. The CDC reports that infertility services have been used by "about 12% of women of childbearing age in the United States."[23] As previously discussed, infertility affects both males and females, and estimates include approximately 15 percent of couples having experience with infertility. So the problem is fairly pervasive. Therefore, we each need to think about it. That raises the issue of how we are to think about infertility biblically and theologically. What guidelines does Scripture offer couples who experience infertility?

CBM: The good news is that there is hope for infertile couples. But first we have to understand why couples often feel traumatized by the experience. One of the "facts of life" is that we were made to procreate. Everything from our biology to our anatomy to our psychology testifies to the "urge to merge" as someone has called it. We are also socialized to procreate. Nearly every young girl is given baby dolls to play with as a child. She grows up imagining what it would be like to be a mother. Even though fewer boys may imagine themselves being a father, by the time we reach reproductive age, the idea begins to have more immediacy. In addition, although the acids of the sexual revolution have eroded the relationship between marriage and procreation, many newly married couples still understand having children as an important part of their future. Often the extended family raises those expectations either by asking things like, "When are you and John going to start a family?" or "You know, your brother and his wife have made us happy grandparents. When are you two going to contribute?" These questions are usually not consciously meant to create anxiety, but if a couple is experiencing infertility, they sometimes feel guilt and self-consciousness. And if other couples within their sphere of relationships are having children, the self-consciousness can be magnified.

Reactions to infertility are often similar to reactions to death. Couples may experience sadness, depression, lowered self-esteem, confused self-image, guilt, anger, grief, and a sense of isolation. This can put tremendous stress on their relationship. Pastors and

---

[23] *2010 Assisted Reproductive Technology Fertility Clinic Success Rates Report*, CDC, American Society for Reproductive Medicine, Society for Assisted Reproductive Technology.

other counselors should be prepared to lead couples through the various stages of grief as couples grapple with infertility.

Ethical Considerations

SANCTITY OF EVERY HUMAN LIFE

When the human egg and sperm unite, a genetically unique individual human being is created. Individuals receive half their genetic identity from their biological mother and half from their biological father. Since every human individual is created in God's image (Gen 1:27), he or she is vested by God with inestimable value. This is what we mean when we refer to the "sanctity" or "sacredness" of every human life. Because of the sanctity of life, technologies that harm humans, even at the embryonic stage, should be avoided.

Some high-tech reproductive technologies do not by themselves violate the sanctity of human life. For example, IVF, DIH, GIFT, and ZIFT do not necessarily require that embryos be destroyed. Yet they do put embryos at risk, especially if combined with embryo freezing. Also, when more than two or three embryos are transferred to a woman's uterus, there is a substantially higher likelihood one or more of those embryos will be put at risk of dying. (These considerations do not diminish concern regarding the risks to the mothers of multiples.)

Another problem associated with the creation of extra embryos is the impossibility of knowing what might happen between the time the embryos are created and the time they are all transferred. In the famous court case *Davis v. Davis* (1992) in Maryville, Tennessee, the Davises used IVF and embryo freezing to try to achieve pregnancy. Embryos were created, and some of them were frozen. Before Mrs. Davis could get pregnant, the couple went through a tumultuous divorce. They disagreed vehemently about what should happen to the frozen embryos. So a suit was filed to decide who would get "custody" of the embryos. By the time the case reached the Tennessee Supreme Court, the embryos were deemed "property" rather than persons. Finally, they were destroyed.

This case underscores how important it is for couples to consider all the possible scenarios they might experience in the course of assisted reproduction. Couples should discuss their religious and moral convictions with their doctor *before* they begin therapy. They should decide how many embryos they believe it is ethical to create.

Once embryos have been made, they cannot be unmade. If they freeze embryos, a decision we cannot endorse, they should determine who would get custody of the embryos should they divorce. They should also determine what would happen to the embryos if one or both of them were to die suddenly.

Other concerns are important as well. For instance, if the husband's sperm is required for assisted reproduction, men are typically given a plastic vial and instructed to donate sperm via masturbation. Pornography is often made available in the clinic to stimulate arousal. Not only does this violate Jesus's command not to lust (Matt 5:28), but it unnecessarily separates a husband and wife from the intimacy of procreation. There is no clinical reason a wife cannot assist her husband in sperm retrieval.

DJR: That is a practical example of "Bible meets fertility clinic." What other theological underpinnings do we need to address regarding the family and procreation?

CBM: There are at least two more.

PRIMACY OF FAMILY IN THE BIBLE

Just as procreation is an aspect of the biblical ideal for the family, so is monogamous, heterosexual marriage. God's ideal for the family is that one man and one woman unite in a one-flesh relationship for life. The apostle Paul points to this ideal when he cites Genesis in his practical instructions on the family in the book of Ephesians: "For this reason a man will leave his father and mother and be joined to his wife, and the two will become one flesh" (Eph 5:31). We all know how traumatic it is when this ideal is violated through adultery, divorce, or even death. Preserving the primacy of the family is increasingly important today, including when considering reproductive technologies.

A number of the reproductive technologies violate God's ideal for the family and are, therefore, rife with difficulties. For instance, surrogate motherhood, one of the more controversial of the reproductive technologies, is contrary to the "nuclear" structure of the family. When a third party intrudes on the procreative relationship, the divinely instituted structure of the family is altered. Trouble is bound to follow.

Abraham and Sarah stand out as important examples of this fact. In fulfillment of his promise to Abraham, God intended to give Abraham and Sarah children—but on God's own timetable, not theirs. In unbelief and impatience Abraham and Sarah decided to introduce a third party into the reproductive relationship. "Sarai said to Abram, 'Since the LORD has prevented me from bearing children, go to my slave; perhaps through her I can build a family'" (Gen 16:2). Sarah offered her servant, Hagar, as a surrogate— a violation of God's ideal for the family. Ishmael was born when Abraham was eighty-six years old. As one might predict, Sarah and Hagar's relationship deteriorated. "Then Sarah mistreated [Hagar] so much that she ran away from her" (Gen 16:6). Heartbreak and disruption of the family resulted. When Abraham was ninety-nine and Sarah was ninety, God caused Sarah to conceive, and she had a son named Isaac. We know the rest of the story.

Commercial surrogacy—where a woman is paid to carry a couple's child to term—is the most objectionable form of surrogacy. This practice commodifies procreation, turning it into a relationship that treats the surrogate as little more than a uterus for hire.

Even so-called altruist surrogacy—where no money is exchanged—is problematic. In pregnancy a maternal-fetal bond is created. In surrogacy cases this bond is broken when, after nine months of carrying the baby in her body, the surrogate must send the child to live with someone else. No one yet knows what the long-term effects will be on the children who are separated from their birth mothers.

Egg donation and artificial insemination using donor sperm ("donor insemination," or DI) also violate God's ideal for the family by creating a child who results from the union of the wife or husband and another person outside the marriage. Unlike adoption, which "redeems" a child who would otherwise not have a family, these arrangements *create* a situation where the parents are not equally related to a child they bring into the world for just such purposes. They also expose children and adults to intensely traumatic challenges, both legal and otherwise.

There is great wisdom in God's design for the family. Social engineering—whether through law, policy, or reproductive technology—is bound to result in damage to men, women, society, and, most importantly, children.

A THEOLOGY OF INFERTILITY

When making procreative decisions, Christians have more than technological questions to ask. Reproductive technologies are not value neutral. That is, just because these technologies are available does not mean they ought to be used or they pass ethical muster. Like all choices, decisions concerning reproductive technology should be informed by a Christian worldview. What does the Bible say about infertility?

First, parenthood is a divine gift and should be celebrated. God ordained procreation for the benefit of humankind. The Bible is pro-natal. In Genesis 1:28, God said: "Be fruitful, multiply, fill the earth, and subdue it." Similarly, the psalmist says: "Sons are indeed a heritage from the LORD, children, a reward. Like arrows in the hand of the warrior are the sons born in one's youth. Happy is the man who has filled his quiver with them" (Ps 127:3–5). Paul wrote, "God sent His Son, born of a woman, born under law, to redeem those under law, so that we might receive adoption as sons" (Gal 4:4-5). God chose to use the procreative process to bring his Son into the world, albeit through the virgin giving birth. And children occupied a special place in Jesus' ministry (see Matt 18:1–6; Mark 10:13–16). Furthermore, one of the believer's relationships to God is defined as a parent-child relationship: "The Spirit Himself testifies together with our spirit that we are God's children, and if children, also heirs—heirs of God and coheirs with Christ" (Rom 8:16–17).

Second, God sovereignly opens and shuts the womb (1 Sam 1:5–6). Although children are indeed a blessing from God, the ability to bear them is subject to the mystery of providence. Thus, the apostle James warns Christians not to be presumptuous about life. Rather than rashly following our own desires, we are taught, "Instead . . . say, '*If the Lord wills*, we will live and do this or that'" (Jas 4:15, emphasis added).

God's providence should not, however, be a dark and foreboding reality for believers. As our Father, he always has his own glory and our best interest at heart, and there is never any real conflict between the two. As Paul taught the Roman Christians, "We know that all things work together for the good of those who love God: those who are called according to His purpose" (Rom 8:28). Although we should not cite the verse flippantly to people who are suffering, the theology of that verse is nonetheless true. God is able to work good out of and through our tragedies and traumas. One of the most assuring realities of the Christian faith is God's *purposefulness*. He never acts capriciously, makes mistakes, or errs in his judgment.

In some cases, for good and gracious reasons, it may not be God's will for a couple to have children. Infertile couples should not be made to feel like second-class humans because they do not have children. God may well have other important purposes for their lives. Sadly, many couples assume infertility is always a sign of God's disfavor or a means of punishment. That is not necessarily the case. At the same time some couples are brought through the experience of infertility before finally conceiving. Of one thing we can be certain, God has promised never to burden us with more than we can bear through his sustaining grace (1 Cor 10:13).

Finally, trials—including infertility—are sometimes brought into the lives of believers as a motivation to pray. Hannah's story in 1 Samuel 1 is a powerful reminder that prayer is often God's appointed means of fulfilling his purposes for us. Hannah was an infertile woman who desperately wanted a child. Her infertility was the source of extreme depression. She prayed so intensely to have a child that the priest thought she might be drunk (1 Sam 1:11–15). Hannah responded to his allegation by saying: "I am a woman with a broken heart. I haven't had any wine or beer; I've been pouring out my heart before the LORD" (v. 15). In time she conceived. Hannah had a son, Samuel, whose name means "heard of God." God answered Hannah's prayers, just as he answers all his children's prayers, by accomplishing his loving purposes in their lives—in this case by giving her a child.

Conclusion

Infertility can be traumatic for couples. The array of reproductive technologies offered can be confusing. Decisions about what technologies to use take enormous mental effort, emotional discipline, and even more spiritual wisdom. Families and friends can help infertile couples as they grapple with the experience by providing the following.

Accurate information. Learn the facts about infertility. Infertility is not necessarily a lifelong condition. Some couples experience years of infertility before having children. Do not give unsolicited advice or share folk remedies. Understand that stories about a family member or friend who was infertile but recently had a baby may not bring comfort to couples in the throes of dealing with their own infertility. Point them to some of the support groups for couples experiencing infertility. For instance, Hannah's Prayer is a Christian support network for infertile couples. And Stepping Stones Ministry in Wichita, Kansas, publishes a newsletter for infertile couples.

Compassionate sensitivity. Special occasions like Mother's Day or baby showers may be difficult for infertile couples. Try to understand why they might not feel comfortable participating on those occasions. When you learn that a couple is experiencing infertility, do not ask, "Oh, whose *fault* is it?" Sometimes couples feel guilty about infertility in the first place. Additional feelings of guilt, either real or imagined, are unlikely to help.

Prayerful support. Support infertile couples by praying for them, pointing them to good resources, and just bearing with them their sense of burden as they seek to trust God and help for their infertility.

Additional Resources

Anonymous Father's Day. DVD. Produced by the Center for Bioethics and Culture, 3380 Vincent Road Ste Hub, Pleasant Hill, CA 94523-4324. Accessed June 30, 2013. http://www.anonymousfathersday.com/about.

Glahn, Sandra, and William Cutrer. *The Infertility Companion: Hope and Help for Couples Facing Infertility.* Grand Rapids, MI: Zondervan, 2004.

Marquardt, Elizabeth, Norval D. Glenn, and Karen Clark. *My Daddy's Name Is Donor: A New Study of Young Adults Conceived Through Sperm Donation.* New York: Institute for American Values, 2010.

Rae, Scott B., and D. Joy Riley. *Outside the Womb: Moral Guidance for Assisted Reproduction.* Chicago: Moody, 2011.

Chapter 6

Organ Donation and Transplantation

Case: "Brother's Transplant Gift
Carries Unbearable Cost"[1]

I don't want you to do it," he told his brother, to which Ryan responded, "You'd do it for me, wouldn't you?"

Chad was willing to wait for a cadaver liver; he did not want his younger brother, Ryan, to donate part of his liver to him. But Chad's disease, primary sclerosing cholangitis (PSC), the cause of which is unknown and for which there is no cure, was progressing quickly. He needed a new liver, but the statistics were against him for a cadaver liver. Each year only about 4,500 cadaver livers become available, while about 16,000 people are usually on the waiting list. No problem, Ryan insisted; he had been tested and was a match. He was willing to donate a portion of his liver to Chad. The transplant should work: living donor liver transplants, where a large portion of the donor's liver is removed, have been done since 1989. This can be done because the liver has the capability to regenerate itself in part: it cannot regenerate itself from nothing

---

[1] Pauline Arrillaga, "Brother's Transplant Gift Carries Unbearable Cost," msnbc.com (updated) November 29 2010, accessed April 16, 2012, http://www.msnbc.msn.com/id /40094048/ns/health-health_care/t/brothers-transplant-gift-carries-unbearable-cost/# .T4wdZI4Yj0A.

but from a portion of liver. So the parts of liver in the donor and the recipient can "regrow" more liver in each. Moreover, the medical center where the surgery was planned had never lost a donor in the liver transplant service, where 141 of the procedures had been done.[2]

The night before the procedure, the family prepared themselves by reading Scripture and taking Communion. They used CaringBridge to keep others informed. Just before Ryan was wheeled away, Chad walked to his room:

> "I owe you my life," he whispered to Ryan, who patted
> Chad on the shoulder and tried, as always, to reassure.
> "Piece of cake," he said.[3]

But it was not a piece of cake, as it turned out. The surgery was a success for both, and Chad began to feel better quickly. Ryan had a harder time of recovery. Saturday, day three after the surgery, was expected to be difficult for the donor, but on day four Ryan suffered a cardiac arrest and was resuscitated. The next day he died.

> "This is how we know what love is: Jesus Christ laid down
> his life for us. And we ought to lay down our lives for our
> brothers."
> —Chad's journal entry called, "1 John 3:16."[4]

What happened? Ryan's autopsy showed a slightly enlarged heart that may have been subject to arrhythmias and the effects of too little oxygen to the brain after the cardiac arrest. His death resulted in a temporary halt in the hospital's transplant program and ultimately resulted in the hospital putting in place measures to monitor donors post-operatively more closely. Chad struggles to live his life in ways that honor his brother's sacrifice. That said, he has made a decision regarding a second transplant, which may be needed.

---

[2] Ibid.

[3] Pauline Arrillaga, "Transplant Recipient Struggles to Go on After Brother's Death," second of a two-part series, msnbc.com, November 15, 2010, accessed April 16, 2012, http://www.msnbc.msn.com/id/40133320/ns/health-health_care/t/transplant-recipient -struggles-go-after-brothers-death/?ns=health-health_care#.T4wiq44Yj0A.

[4] Ibid.

The one thing he can control: He refuses to ever again accept a live donation; the responsibility is just too great. "If Ryan hadn't done what he did, I'd be dead," he says. "I'm not going to put that on anybody else. If I don't make it waiting for a cadaver, I'd rather have that than to have anything else."[5]

Questions for Reflection

1. Is organ donation/transplantation consistent with a Christian theology of the integrity of the body?

2. Is organ donation a moral duty? What about where family is concerned? In this case, is Ryan his brother's keeper?

3. What biblical norms or principles ought to be considered before reaching a decision in this case?

4. What should Christians do, if anything, to encourage organ donation?

Discussion

C. Ben Mitchell (CBM): Organ donation and transplantation is a relatively new innovation in medicine. The first successful human transplant took place only a little over sixty years ago when a kidney was transplanted from Ronald Herrick into his twin brother, Richard. But that's not where the idea of organ transplantation began. Dr. Riley, tell us a bit about the history of transplantation.

D. Joy Riley (DJR): The ancients understood the importance of bodily organs. For instance, when the Egyptians mummified bodies, most internal organs were removed, preserved in salt, wrapped

---

[5] Ibid.

in linen, and stored in jars with lids signifying gods who would watch over them. The lungs, liver, stomach, and intestines were so treated but not the heart. Neither the kidneys nor the heart was removed, the latter being considered the seat of the person's thought and will. The brain, however, was apparently considered less important, as it was removed (via the nose) and discarded.[6]

Increased understanding of anatomy and physiology and the addition of anesthesiology to surgery brought many changes in medicine. Although a kidney was the first organ transplanted—in 1954—a heart transplant in 1967 garnered worldwide excitement. In the words of Dr. Christiaan Barnard: "On Saturday, I was a surgeon in South Africa, very little known. On Monday I was world renowned."[7] He subsequently pioneered a number of other treatments, including "joining a healthy heart to the patient's to create a 'double pump', designing artificial heart valves and using monkeys' hearts to keep alive desperately ill people."[8]

The first heart transplant in the United States was performed the following year, in Virginia. In May 1968, an African-American laborer, fifty-six-year-old Bruce Tucker, fell and experienced a "massive brain injury." Surgery was done to relieve pressure on his brain, and he was placed on a ventilator. His treating physician was not optimistic, however, reckoning that Tucker's "prognosis for recovery is nil and death imminent."[9] A day after the accident, an electroencephalogram (EEG) showed "flat lines with occasional artifact"—interpreted as no cortical (higher brain) activity.[10] Two hours and thirty-five minutes later, Mr. Tucker was taken to the operating room, his ventilator turned off, and five minutes later was declared dead. During those five minutes an incision was made in the recipient, Joseph Klett, readying him for Bruce Tucker's heart. Mr. Tucker died that day; Mr. Klett, about a week later.[11]

---

[6] "Quest for Immortality: Treasures of Ancient Egypt" exhibition brochure (Nashville, TN: Frist Center for the Visual Arts, 2006). Accessed 30 June 2013. More information can be found at http://nashville.about.com/od/culturalarts/a/frist_egypt.htm.

[7] "Christiaan Barnard: Single-Minded Surgeon," *BBC News*, September 2, 2001, accessed April 11, 2012, http://news.bbc.co.uk/1/hi/health/1470356.stm.

[8] Ibid.

[9] Robert M. Veatch, *Transplantation Ethics* (Washington, DC: Georgetown University Press, 2000), 43.

[10] Ibid.

[11] Ibid., 43–44.

William E. Tucker, brother of the deceased, brought suit, charging that this was a "nefarious scheme" to use his brother's heart, that his death had been hastened by turning off the ventilator, and that "the removal of organs was carried out with only minimal attempts to notify the victim's family and obtain permission for his organs."[12] The jury found in favor of the physicians, and the case was reported in the media as a "brain death" case.[13]

Definition of Death

In July of that same year, the *Journal of the American Medical Association (JAMA)*, published the so-called Harvard Criteria for "irreversible coma." The committee, which included "physicians, lawyers, theologians, and social scientists," enumerated the criteria for irreversible coma as:

1. Unreceptivity and unresponsivity
2. No movement/breathing
3. No reflexes
4. Flat EEG[14]

These tests had to be reproducible after a specified time period (usually twenty-four to forty-eight hours, depending on the age of the patient and the state's laws) in order for the diagnosis to stand. This definition ultimately constituted a new definition of *death*: "brain death."

CBM: So it was in the context of the debates surrounding organ transplantation that we got our current definition of brain death, often understood as a "flat line" or "flat EEG." What was the previous definition of *death*?

DJR: Prior to this the accepted definition of *death* had been the cessation of lung and heart function; that is, it was a cardiopulmonary definition. Death was pronounced when the patient stopped breathing and his or her heart stopped beating. After the Harvard Criteria were established, "irreversible coma" or "brain death" became another official way of determining when someone was

---

[12] Ibid., 44.
[13] Ibid., 45.
[14] Ibid., 46.

dead. New laws had to be written to cover this new category of death.

The American Medical Association (AMA) and the American Bar Association (ABA) each had interests in consistent laws among states. Therefore, the Uniform Determination of Death Act (UDDA) was written in 1980, and most states have enacted it. The UDDA says: "An individual who has sustained either (1) irreversible cessation of circulatory and respiratory functions, or (2) irreversible cessation of all functions of the entire brain, including the brain stem, is dead. A determination of death must be made in accordance with accepted medical standards."[15]

CBM: Since 1981, then, a person could be declared dead by either brain death criteria or by cardiopulmonary criteria. Did that end the debate?

DJR: By no means! As time has passed, questions have arisen. Must brain death include the "whole brain"—including the brainstem—or can it just involve the neocortex, the "higher brain," seen as responsible for integration of the person?

In recent years the definition has been stretched further. Organs from so-called "non-heart-beating cadavers" have been increasingly employed in transplantation. In these cases ventilator-dependent people who have "no hope of recovery" (and with appropriate consent) are taken to the OR, and their ventilators are turned off. Although they are not "brain dead," they are declared dead by cardiopulmonary criteria; and after a period of some minutes (from two to five, depending on the protocol), organ recovery, or "harvesting," begins. This is called the donation after cardiac death protocol (DCD). How long does the heart have to be stopped before death is declared? How long does the ventilator have to be turned off? Why is this important?

These are crucial questions not least because death triggers a number of events in our lives, as Robert M. Veatch points out so well in his book *Transplantation Ethics*. Death tells us it is time to mourn the passing of a fellow human, be that a family member, friend, or other. Wills are read and worldly goods disseminated.

---

[15] "Uniform Determination of Death Act," accessed April 12, 2012, http://www.law.upenn.edu/bll/archives/ulc/fnact99/1980s/udda80.htm.

Titles are changed. Leadership is handed over to other, living persons. At death bodies and their organs are no longer needed by the previously alive. If the organs are in sufficiently healthy condition, they can be transplanted into those who need better functioning versions. Veatch says that death is a "philosophical or moral question, not a medical or scientific one."[16] In Veatch's terms it is a question of rights. Living people have them; the dead do not.

CBM: The importance of a correct definition of death cannot be overstated, especially from the perspective of the Christian faith. Removing someone's life-sustaining organs before they are dead would be a form of homicide. The Sixth Commandment is "Do not murder" (Exod 20:13). To end the life of another person unjustly, or prematurely, is a terrible offense. Furthermore, since Christians affirm the immortality of the soul and—to cite the Apostles' Creed—"the resurrection of the body: and the life everlasting," death becomes a critical event bridging this life and the life to come. Getting the definition of death right is critical.

Of course, prior to the invention of contemporary medical technologies like ventilators and EKG machines, the only way death could be determined was when breathing and heartbeat stopped. Brain death criteria introduced something entirely new. Now, through mechanical supports, breathing and heartbeat can be maintained, in some cases seemingly indefinitely, despite the fact that the part of the brain that processes information ceases to function. Not only has this redefined death, but it has also made possible such a diagnosis as "persistent vegetative state" (PVS).

The new definition of death introduces a couple of problems. First, it seems to make what is going on inside the head the only thing that is important about life and living, death and dying. Is the human brain the locus of life? If so, is the human brain the seat of the soul? Those are crucial questions. Second, occasionally, someone who was diagnosed to be in a PVS condition, recovers the ability to communicate. In 2012, for instance, Steven Thorpe, then seventeen, was declared by four doctors to be brain dead following a motor vehicle accident in England. His parents were told that they needed to begin thinking about organ donation. Steven's father asked for another opinion. Julia Piper, a private-practice GP

---

[16] Veatch, *Transplantation Ethics*, 46.

from West Midlands, detected that, however faint, Steven did have brain activity. Today, Steven is fully recovered and at age twenty-one was a trainee-accountant.[17] Though rare, examples like this can be multiplied. So getting the definition of death right is important.

Has there been sufficient debate among the public? Not according to physicians like Paul Byrne, MD, the past president of the Catholic Health Association. Dr. Byrne claims there are more than 175 known long-term survivors of brain death.[18] If true, this would mean that a brain-death diagnosis is less than accurate. In January 2009, the President's Council on Bioethics, under the leadership of the distinguished clinician and medical ethicist Edmund Pellegrino, MD, issued a white paper called, "Controversies in the Determination of Death." Dr. Pellegrino suggested in his synopsis that, even among the experts, the jury is still out:

> After reviewing the relevant literature and the testimony of many experts, followed by intensive discussion between and among its members, the Council has concluded that the neurological standard remains valid. Some Council members, however, believe that a better philosophical rationale than the one proposed by the President's Commission of 1981 should be adopted. A few Council members argue that there is sufficient uncertainty about the neurological standard to warrant an alternative approach to the care of the "brain dead" human being and the question of organ procurement.[19]

Organ Donation

Once death has been determined, how does the organ donation system work in America? Given that there are always fewer life-saving organs available than the number of patients who need them, how do we know they are distributed equitably?

---

[17] Hannah Furness, "'Miracle Recovery' of Teen Declared Brain Dead by Four Doctors," *The Telegraph*, April 25, 2012, accessed June 30, 2013, http://www.telegraph.co.uk/health /healthnews/9223408/Miracle-recovery-of-teen-declared-brain-dead-by-four-doctors.html.

[18] Catholic Free Press, "Doctor Disputes Common Acceptance of 'Brain Death,'" November 15, 2012, accessed June 11, 2013, http://www.catholicfreepress.org/lead-story-2/2012/11/15 /doctor-disputes-common-acceptance-of-%E2%80%98brain-death%E2%80%99.

[19] Edmund D. Pellegrino, Letter of Transmittal, *Controversies in the Determination of Death* (Washington, DC: President's Council on Bioethics, 2009), accessed June 30, 2013, http://bioethics.georgetown.edu/pcbe/reports/death/transmittal.html.

DJR: In 1968, the Uniform Anatomical Gift Act (UAGA) created a legal right to donate organs and tissues, whether one's own or someone else's. In 1984 the National Organ Transplant Act (NOTA) made it illegal for anyone to sell or acquire an organ for "valuable consideration." So in the United States organs cannot be bought or sold legally, and people have the ability to decide in advance what happens with their organs.

What organs may be transplanted? There are several, and these are codified in law:

> "Human organ," as covered by section 301 of the National Organ Transplant Act, as amended, means the human (including fetal) kidney, liver, heart, lung, pancreas, bone marrow, cornea, eye, bone, skin, and intestine, including the esophagus, stomach, small and/or large intestine, or any portion of the gastrointestinal tract.[20]

How does the organ donation system work? Formally, we have what is referred to as an "opt-in" system. That is, one may actively decide to donate one's organs (or, under certain circumstances, the organs of a loved one). Designation of oneself as a donor can be done on the driver's license. A less formal but important act is to inform one's closest family members of the decision to be an organ donor, for, by law, they will be asked about donation when the time comes.

CBM: So the next of kin is always approached about organs when someone dies?

DJR: That is usually the case, but if the driver's license has been signed designating the signee as a donor, no other approval is necessary.

CBM: That is not common knowledge, I think.

---

[20] Electronic Code of Federal Regulations, Title 42: Public Health, § 121.13, Definition of Human Organ Under Section 301 of the National Organ Transplant Act, as amended, accessed April 16, 2012, http://ecfr.gpoaccess.gov/cgi/t/text/text-idx?c=ecfr& sid=16ca5ffa7ab78548b2ba7415350400b3&rgn=div8&view=text&node=42:1.0.1.11.78.0 .39.13&idno=42.

DJR: You are right about that, and it is important. It is also important to understand the different systems of organ donation.

The opposite of an "opt-in" system is an "opt-out" system, where the state effectively has control over one's organs after death unless the person has completed the necessary measures for "opting out," defined by that country's laws. As will be seen later in this chapter, our policies are being increasingly modified toward an opt-out system.

Another development in 1984 was the institution of the Organ Procurement Organizations (OPOs) and the Organ Procurement and Transplantation Network (OPTN). Through the Department of Health and Human Services (DHHS; now simply, HHS) and the Health Resources and Services Administration (HRSA), the federal government carved out fifty-eight regional OPOs, which employ organ procurement officers, and a number of others to facilitate the obtaining of organs for transplantation. These OPOs and their employees are being given increasing roles in the procurement of organs for transplantation. A nonprofit organization, the United Network for Organ Sharing (UNOS), is contracted by the government to oversee the distribution of organs.

How are potential organ donors identified? The "Patient Self-Determination Act" (PSDA) became effective in December 1991. According to the PSDA, patients have the right to participate in and direct health-care decisions, the right to accept or refuse medical interventions, and the right to prepare advance directives and living wills. Advance directives can include one's desires regarding organ donation as well as the disposition of the body after death. By the same law, providers have to implement certain policies in order to assure that patients' rights are exercised. Whenever you are admitted to a hospital, for instance, you will be asked if you have prepared advance directives, and if not, you will be offered assistance in doing so. You are not required to fill out advance directives, but the hospital or nursing home is required to ask you if you wish to do so. The options for advance directives are several and are covered elsewhere in this book. Advance directives, however, can set the stage for the donation of organs.

Another way potential donors are identified is through what is called "required request" policies. In order to receive Medicare and Medicaid reimbursement, hospitals must notify organ recovery agencies of all patient deaths, and properly trained persons must speak with the families of the deceased about organ donation. According to a 1998 policy of the US Department of Health and Human Services:

> A hospital must contact the [Organ Procurement Organization] by telephone as soon as possible after an individual has died, has been placed on a ventilator due to a severe brain injury, or who has been declared brain dead (ideally within 1 hour). That is, a hospital must notify the OPO while a brain dead or severely brain-injured, ventilator-dependent individual is still attached to the ventilator and as soon as possible after the death of any other individual, including a potential non-heart-beating donor. Even if the hospital does not consider an individual who is not on a ventilator to be a potential donor, the hospital must call the OPO as soon as possible after the death of that individual has occurred.[21]

CBM: I find it interesting that reimbursement is tied to required request for organs.

DJR: I find it both interesting and sobering. That covers much about donation of organs. Let's turn now to transplantation.

Organ Transplantation in the United States

Most donations are cadaver donations; that is, organs are donated after a person's death. In fact, death of the donor is an important part of organ donation and transplantation, at least in the situation of unpaired organs, such as hearts. "Since its inception, organ transplantation has been guided by the overarching ethical requirement known as the dead donor rule, which simply states that patients must be declared dead before the removal of any vital organs for transplantation."[22] There is an important second part of that rule:

---

[21] Department of Health and Human Services, Centers for Medicare and Medicaid Services, CMS Manual System, Pub 100-07 State Operations Provider Certification, Transmittal 37, October17, 2008, R37SOMA.pdf, 309–70, accessed April 16, 2012, http://www.cms.gov/transmittals/downloads/R37SOMA.pdf.

[22] Robert D. Truog and Franklin G. Miller, "The Dead Donor Rule and Organ Transplantation," *New England Journal of Medicine* 359, no. 7, August 14, 2008: 674–75, accessed April 23, 2010, http://content.nejm.org/cgi/content/full/359/7/674?query=TOC.

the procurement, the obtaining, of the organ cannot cause the death of the donor. This second portion of the dead donor rule applies to all donors.

Although most donations in the US are cadaver donations, donations can come from living donors, as well. Living donors can donate one of a paired set of organs (like one kidney); a lobe of liver; or part of a lung, the pancreas, or intestine to relatives (living, related), non-blood-related family or friends (living, unrelated), or strangers (anonymous). Sometimes paired organ donations are arranged. An example of that would be two married couples, with one spouse from each couple needing a kidney, and the other spouse willing to donate a kidney, but not being a good match, in terms of blood group compatibility. So a swap of compatible donor-recipient organs is arranged, whereby Donor Spouse X gives a kidney to Recipient Spouse Z, and Donor Spouse Z gives a kidney to Recipient Spouse X. This is relatively rare but does occur.

As of May 2008, the United States had 254 transplant centers.

> 245 kidney transplant programs
> 127 liver transplant programs
> 146 pancreas transplant programs
> 29 pancreas islet cell programs
> 45 intestine transplant programs
> 130 heart transplant programs
> 52 heart-lung transplant programs
> 65 lung transplant programs
> 839 total number of transplant programs[23]

In 2012, 28,053 organ transplants were done in the US. Most of these represented organs from deceased donors (22,187).[24]

CBM: If someone needs a transplant, how are they identified? Since there is always a waiting list for lifesaving organs, who decides which patient gets the next available organ?

---

[23] *Partnering with Your Transplant Team* 2008; PartneringWithTransplantTeam_508v.pdf, 9, accessed April 16, 2012, http://www.ask.hrsa.gov/detail_materials.cfm?ProdID=3401.

[24] HHS/HRSA/OPTN Organ Procurement and Transplantation Network, "Transplants by Donor Type," accessed February 6, 2014, http://optn.transplant.hrsa.gov/latestData /rptData.asp.

DJR: UNOS is incorporated as a private, nonprofit organization that works under contract with the federal government to manage the nation's organ transplant system. Since 1986 they have done so through the OPTN, which operates according to federal regulations. Employed organ procurement officers are now an integral part of the system. UNOS maintains a website where the number of potential organ recipients is prominently displayed. On April 11, 2012, the number of waiting list candidates was 113,830. The "active" waiting list candidates numbered significantly fewer, at 72,697.[25] Physicians add patient names to the waiting list when certain criteria relating to illness severity and transplant need are reached. Who receives a transplant, and when, is based on a variety of factors. Some of these are level of need (manifested by place on the transplant list), the organ needed, the availability of a matched organ, and locale. Locale matters because organs have a limited time (in hours, typically) they can be outside the body and still be used for transplantation. Additionally, not every locale has a transplant center. UNOS coordinates these logistics and more regarding who gets a transplant and when.

The following diagram gives an overview of the relationships between HHS, OPOs, and hospitals. HHS sets goals and regulates both OPOs and hospitals (see page 142).

Under the rubric of the current system in the United States, hospitals that receive Medicare or Medicaid funding, or other small "critical access hospitals," must have in place a written contract with the local OPO. Additionally, these hospitals must also have in place a donation after cardiac death (DCD) protocol. By federal regulation the hospital must notify the OPO of the impending or actual death of a patient. The certified procurement coordinator is the person who may discuss organ donation with a patient or family/next of kin/surrogate; the physician is forbidden from initiating this discussion. Under what is termed the "presumptive approach," the OPO coordinator is trained to introduce him/herself as a member of the medical team, when, in fact, that person has no care responsibilities for the patient.[26]

---

[25] UNOS, accessed June 12, 2012, http://www.unos.org.

[26] Robert D. Truog, "When Does a Nudge Become a Shove in Seeking Consent for Organ Donation?," *The American Journal of Bioethics* 12, no. 2, February 2012: 42–44.

HHS Regulation of Organ Procurement

2003 - The HHS initiates organ donation breakthough collaborative goal: Hospitals to reach target of ≥ 75% cadaveric organ donation

Organ Procurement Organizations
(OPOs) originally established in 1984

1) 58 Regional OPOs in US
2) Must be notified of impending or actual death of a patient by hospital
3) Only the certified procurement coordinator (OPO employee) can initiate discussion of organ donation with potential donor and/or family

UAGA

Hospitals

1) Required to have a contract with an OPO
2) Required to have DCD protocol in place
3) Required to notify OPO of impending or actual death of patient
4) The default rule is to initiate/continue life support to preserve organs until the patient is evaluated for organ donation

Laws, like the UAGA, impact all citizens. According to the OPTN website:

> The 1968 Uniform Anatomical Gift Act (UAGA) provided the legal foundation upon which human organs and tissues could be donated for transplantation by execution of an anatomical gift authorizing document. Since 1972, all 50 states and the District of Columbia have adopted this Act, or amended forms of this Act.[27]

CBM: The Uniform Anatomical Gift Act was revised in 2006. How has that changed the landscape?

DJR: You are aware that I am not a lawyer, and I do not claim to understand all the ramifications of the law. Some concern has been expressed, however, about this revision. Verheijde, Rady, and McGregor published an article in 2007 detailing theirs:

> The Revised UAGA (2006) poses challenges to the Patient Self-Determination Act (PSDA) embodied in advance health care directives and individual expression about the use of life support systems at the end-of-life. The challenges are predicated on the UAGA revising the default choice to *presumption of donation intent* and the use of life support systems to ensure medical suitability of organs for transplantation. The default choice trumps the expressed intent in an individual's advance health care directive to withhold and/or withdraw life support systems at the end-of-life. The Revised UAGA (2006) overrides advance directives on utilitarian grounds, which is a serious ethical challenge to society. The subtle progression of the Revised UAGA (2006) towards the presumption about how to dispose of one's organs at death can pave the way for an affirmative "duty to donate."[28]

---

[27] HRSA/OPTN Resources, Entry *Uniform Anatomical Gift Act*, "Glossary," accessed February 5, 2014, http://optn.transplant.hrsa.gov/resources/glossary.asp#U.

[28] Joseph L. Verheijde, Mohamed Y. Rady, and Joan L. McGregor, "The United States Revised Uniform Anatomical Gift Act (2006): New challenges to balancing patient rights and physician responsibilities," *Philosophy, Ethics, and Humanities in Medicine* 2 (2007): 19, accessed February 6, 2014, http://www.ncbi.nlm.nih.gov/pmc/articles/PMC2001294.

Additionally, the amended UAGA provides for minors to be able to donate organs through checking the box on their driver's licenses. The UAGA as amended also enlarges the pool of persons who can donate another's organs and allows OPOs to gain access to patient medical records, donor registries, and motor vehicle department records. Furthermore, there is now a default rule of the initiation or continuation of life support for organ preservation until the patient is evaluated as a potential organ donor. Such life support may include, among other things, a ventilator and the placement of large catheters for bypass machines or extracorporeal membrane oxygenation (ECMO). Anticoagulants may be administered, and procedures such as a bronchoscopy may be done; these are not therapeutic for the patient but done for the benefit of the recipient. Another concern (although this is related to the regulations as written and not the UAGA) is the restriction that the patient not be charged for any of these procedures/provisions has been removed.[29] Usually, however, once the decision to donate has been made, the OPO (and therefore, tax dollars) covers the cost of organ procurement.

CBM: This is all informative about the way the organ donation/transplantation system works in the American context. Important ethical questions arise in light of this data.

Interestingly, most religious traditions—Judaism, Christianity, Islam, Buddhism, Hinduism, and others—favor organ donation and transplantation under appropriate circumstances.[30] Indeed, from a Christian perspective organ donation can be seen as an extension of neighbor love (Mark 12:30–31). Especially if, after death, you are no longer in need of your organs and they can either save the life of or improve the quality of life of someone else, it seems laudatory to donate your organs. Organ donation is viewed in this case as an act of Christian charity.

---

[29] *At-a-Glance*: "Proposal to Update and Clarify Language in the DCD Model Elements; Affected/Proposed Bylaw: Attachment III to Appendix B of the OPTN Bylaws," 10, accessed February 5, 2014, http://optn.transplant.hrsa.gov/PublicComment/pubcommentPropSub_283.pdf; *OPTN Organ Procurement and Transplantation Network Bylaws*, effective, February 1, 2014; accessed February 5, 2014, http://optn.transplant.hrsa.gov/ContentDocuments/OPTN_Bylaws.pdf.

[30] See http://www.thenationalnetworkoforgandonors.org/religion-and-organ-donation.html.

For instance, in 2000 the late Pope John Paul II said in his encyclical *Evangelium Vitae* that one way of nurturing a culture of life "is the donation of organs, performed in an ethically acceptable manner, with a view to offering a chance of health and even of life itself to the sick who sometimes have no other hope."[31] Furthermore, the nation's largest non-Catholic religious denomination, the Southern Baptist Convention, passed a resolution in 1988 stating that "we encourage voluntarism regarding organ donations in the spirit of stewardship, compassion for the needs of others, and alleviating suffering."[32] Even Jehovah's Witnesses, who staunchly oppose blood transfusions, favor organ donation as long as the blood is first removed from the organs before transplantation.[33]

DJR: I concur with these advocates of altruistic organ donation and urge that our procedures for procurement and transplantation be done in "an ethically acceptable manner," as written by Pope John Paul II. My point in elucidating the above concerns is to point out the opportunities for sliding into unethical practices and producing harm instead of the good that is desired on the part of those who craft the laws and regulations, those who perform or facilitate the transplants, and those who donate or receive organs. Indeed, the entire citizenry is affected; we bear responsibility, beyond the regulations, to be one another's "keeper." I would argue, and I think you would agree, that this applies not only to organs but also to ethics.

Another issue we need to consider is a market for organs. Some have called for a market in organs as a way to increase the supply. What are your thoughts?

CBM: Monetary, or other incentives, compromise the principle of voluntary consent. For instance, in India it is permissible to sell a kidney. In 2002, the average amount received by a donor for his or her kidney was $1,070 US. According to a study in the *JAMA*,

---

[31] *Evangelium Vitae*, paragraph 86, http://www.vatican.va/holy_father/john_paul_ii/encyclicals/documents/hf_jp-ii_enc_25031995_evangelium-vitae_en.html.

[32] Southern Baptist Convention, Resolution on Human Organ Donations, June 1988, http://www.sbc.net/resolutions/amResolution.asp?ID=791.

[33] "There Is No Biblical Command Pointedly Forbidding the Taking in of Other Human Tissue. It Is a Matter for Personal Decision," *Watchtower*, March 15, 1980, 31.

96 percent of participants sold their kidneys to pay off debts. The results were not encouraging:

- Average family income declined by one-third after nephrectomy, and the number of participants living below the poverty line increased.
- Three-fourths of participants were still in debt at the time of the survey.
- About 86 percent of participants reported deterioration in their health status after nephrectomy.
- Seventy-nine percent would not recommend that others sell a kidney.[34]

It certainly appears that those who sold their kidneys were worse off after doing so than they were before they sold their organs. Moreover, poverty and indebtedness made the offer of payment for organ almost irresistible. In other words, money became a coercive influence. From these data we have every reason to think that it would, in fact, be the poor who would be most at risk of abuse in a system where compensation was offered for organ donation.

DJR: That is rather telling, isn't it? The stories of the 2004 tsunami victims selling their kidneys in hopes of finding a way forward from the devastation are particularly moving.[35] My heart wrenches as I think about this study and the probable effects of their sacrifices.

We seem to have covered much of interest in the area of organ donation and transplantation. Is anything more needed?

CBM: Beyond all of the issues already covered, there is the important concern of body integrity. Some Christians may worry that organ donation might be a problem because it disturbs the integrity of the body. The question is sometimes posed: What happens to donated organs in the resurrection? If the organs from one body are distributed into a number of other bodies, what does this mean for the resurrection of the donor? The answer, of course, is that the resurrected body will be so different from the organic, natural body, that this will not be a problem. For instance, no one suggests that

---

[34] M. Goyal et al., "Economic and Health Consequences of Selling a Kidney in India," *Journal of the American Medical Association* 288, no. 13 (2002): 1589–93.

[35] TN Gopalan, "Tsunami victims 'selling kidneys,'" *BBC News*, January 16, 2007, accessed February 5, 2014, http://news.bbc.co.uk/2/hi/south_asia/6266641.stm.

those whose bodies are maimed or even disintegrated in catastrophic circumstances pose a problem in the resurrection. The hope of the resurrection is that even those whose bodies have been destroyed by death or disaster will be raised incorruptible (1 Cor 15:12–58)!

Having said this, however, organ donation/transplantation raises important justice questions. First, are our organs our individual property? Do we own them like we own a house or a car? If so, for how long? Are our organs ours only as long as we live? If not, who owns them after we die? Does the state have an interest in our organs? Should it? How are donor organs allocated? Is any coercion involved?

Of the many religious traditions that favor organ donation, most do so as long as it is consistent with the individual's conscience and there is no coercion. In other words, as long as the individual *freely* consents, organ donation is *permissible*. In no religion is donation *obligatory*. The emphasis is on the freedom to donate or not donate according to one's conscience. So any form of coercion would make donation questionable at best and unethical at worst. The problem of coercion is why, thus far, we have preserved an opt-in, nonpayment system in the United States. Both "presumed consent" and paying for organs are viewed as forms of coercion.

Conclusion

Organ transplantation has been a life-giving and life-sustaining development in modern medicine. Donation can be a poignant example of loving one's neighbor. But donation/transplantation should not be approached naively. In our view organ donation must remain absolutely voluntary and no financial incentives should be permitted. Organ donation should remain a matter of conscience where donor organs are only retrieved through the free and informed consent of the donor. Additionally, we view the dead donor rule as a good rule and see no reason to jettison it.

Although we favor organ donation in principle, we think appropriate safeguards must be erected to ensure that donation is free and uncoerced. We also worry that shifting definitions of death make it increasingly likely that important ethical boundaries will be breeched in organ transplantation. This would be unfortunate for the future of organ donation in the United States and beyond.

Additional Resources

Rose, Daniel Asa. *Larry's Kidney*. New York: William Morrow, 2009.

Smith, Wesley J. *Culture of Death: The Assault on Medical Ethics in America*. New York: Encounter Books, 2000.

Younger, Stuart J., Robert M. Arnold, and Renie Schapiro, eds. *The Definition of Death: Contemporary Controversies*. Baltimore, MD: The Johns Hopkins University Press, 1999.

Chapter 7

Clones and Human-Animal Hybrids

Case: Oregon Stem-cell Groundbreaker Stirs International Frenzy with Cloning Advance[1]

Human cloning is a polarizing subject. The concept has been around for decades, and in recent years the research has intermittently sent shivers down spines. These shivering attacks have often been followed by retractions and embarrassment, but it is not clear that such will always be the case. Stunning the world in May 2013 was the work led by Shoukhrat Mitalipov, at the Oregon Health and Science University (OHSU).

Mitalipov, originally from Kazakhstan, now resides in Portland, Oregon. He was hired away from his previous position at Utah because of his "skills with high-powered microscopes and delicate instruments to move the nucleus of one cell into another."[2] His work, like that of the prominent cloning scientists to date, was begun in animals (in this case, monkeys), and the techniques were then transferred to humans. The OHSU primate lab and the fact that OHSU allows researchers to pay women for donated eggs, are

---

[1] Nick Budnick, "Oregon Stem-cell Groundbreaker Stirs International Frenzy with Cloning Advance," *The Oregonian*, June 2, 2013, accessed June 18, 2013, http://www .oregonlive.com/health/index.ssf/2013/06/oregon_stem-cell_groundbreaker.html.

[2] Ibid.

both components of Mitalipov's success to date, according to writer Nick Budnick.

Here is Budnick's description of Mitalipov at work:

> The cell manipulation machines use computer-aided imaging to allow manipulation of things the width of a micron—one-millionth of a meter.
>
> Mitalipov uses them to strip the nucleus from an egg and replace it with DNA from a skin cell. His team activates the cell using chemicals, electricity, and caffeine—one of Mitalipov's special twists.
>
> The result is what biologists call an early embryo, formed using cloning techniques, although unfertilized.
>
> Then stem cells are extracted from the embryo and grown into bunches scrunched together like the core of a pomegranate. Thousands of stem cells are stored in a translucent plastic vial the size of a short, fat cigarette, then frozen in liquid nitrogen.
>
> The stem cells produced are an identical match to the skin-cell donor, making them ideal for transplants and personalized therapies. Some scientists disagree, but Mitalipov says his are higher quality stem cells than a competing technology that does not destroy embryos.[3]

Questions for Reflection

1. Should we clone human beings? Why or why not?

2. Should we clone animals? Why or why not?

3. Should we mix animal and human DNA?

4. Does the potential for treatments and cures justify creating human embryos for research?

5. What biblical norms or principles, if any, ought to be considered before reaching a decision in this case?

---

[3] Ibid.

✛

Discussion

D. Joy Riley (DJR): When Dolly the cloned sheep stepped onto the world's stage in 1997, she was greeted with cheers as well as a collective gasp. The successful cloning of one mammal meant it might be possible to clone humans. The stuff of science fiction was on the verge of becoming science fact.

Dolly's existence was made possible by a number of important historical developments. A brief rehearsal of those events will help clarify some of the issues involved.

Cloning refers to the asexual reproduction of an organism through embryo splitting (identical twins are an example), or through somatic cell nuclear transfer (SCNT). SCNT is the primary method of cloning employed currently. In SCNT the nucleus of an egg, which contains the majority of an animal's genetic material, is removed. The egg is then referred to as "enucleated." The nucleus of a somatic cell (a body cell, not a sperm or egg) is removed and placed inside the enucleated egg. Since the newly resident nucleus came from a somatic cell, the egg now contains the full complement of chromosomes from the original adult cell. An electrical or chemical stimulus is applied, and if successful, the egg begins to divide as if it had been fertilized. The cloned embryo is incubated and then transferred to a hormonally prepared uterus for gestation. The procedure is not efficient—at least not yet. Dolly was the result of 277 eggs undergoing SCNT. The first 276 were apparently failures at some point in the process. Finally, Dolly was born.

Donald Bruce, director of the Church of Scotland's Society, Religion, and Technology Project, explained the advent of Dolly in this way in his 1997 essay, "A View from Edinburgh":

> Many are wondering how our God-given abilities have apparently brought us to the verge of photocopying ourselves—without our even noticing it. This has added force to a growing undercurrent of concern across Western Europe about how few people have any say about the way in which biotechnology is being allowed to develop. Have

we allowed the imaginations of those to whom society entrusts this particular expression of the image of God to become too free, set loose from their ethical and social moorings? . . .

From the point of view of animal genetics and embryology, Dolly was the result of a natural progression of ideas, each step seen as a logical progression from the previous one. This is the phenomenon sometimes known as "gradualism." It is notoriously difficult to realize the full ethical import of the complete series of steps, until suddenly one of them produces something as tangible as a live sheep cloned from an udder cell, and we wake up abruptly to something that has been happening imperceptibly.[4]

"Imperceptibly" is an appropriate term for what had been going on for decades in the realm of cloning and related technologies. A committee was established in the early 1980s in the U.K. to advise Parliament about assisted reproductive technologies in the wake of the 1978 birth of Louise Joy Brown, the first "test-tube baby." The committee's assignment was: "To consider recent and potential developments in medicine and science related to human fertilization and embryology; to consider what policies and safeguards should be applied, including consideration of the social, ethical, and legal implications of these developments; and to make recommendations." This committee was named for its most famous member and the chair of the committee, Baroness Mary Warnock, a distinguished philosopher. The deliberations of the Warnock Committee included the subjects of cloning and "nucleus substitution." The Warnock Report, published in 1984, noted successful cloning in other species, but not in humans, and described nucleus substitution as a possible source of organs for transplantation.

It has been suggested that one day it might be possible to produce immunologically identical organs for transplantation purposes to replace a diseased organ, for example a kidney. The cloned replacement organ would be grown in an embryo in which the nucleus had been replaced by one

---

[4] Donald M. Bruce, "A View from Edinburgh," in *Human Cloning*, ed. Ronald Cole-Turner (Louisville, KY: WJK, 1997), 3.

taken from the person for whom the replacement organ was intended.[5]

Conclusions reached by the committee were far from unanimous; in fact, many recommendations were the work of a narrow majority. It is instructive that the idea of cloning through nuclear replacement (then called nucleus substitution) was part of that discussion. Indeed, that committee argued that the embryo "might legitimately be used as a means to an end that was good for other humans, both now and in the future," including for research.[6]

The Warnock Committee noted that the embryo, *per se*, had no legal status, and so there was no law protecting the embryo's right to life.[7] Even so, the committee agreed there should be some respect for the embryo, and "no one should undertake research on human embryos the purposes of which could be achieved by the use of other animals or in some other way."[8] Several restrictions on embryo research were recommended by the Warnock Committee:

1. Endpoint of research on embryos was set at 14 days post-fertilisation (not including freezer time).
2. Embryos used for research should never be transferred to a woman.
3. "Disposal" of embryos ("spare" embryos used for research or to be discarded) should be done only with the "informed consent of the couple for whom that embryo was generated."[9]

The committee recommended, and Parliament approved, establishing a licensing body to deal with gametes (eggs or sperm) and embryos: the Human Fertilisation and Embryologic Authority (HFEA).

In 1996, the British Human Genetics Advisory Commission (HGAC) was established in order to "take a broad view of developments in human genetics and advise on ways to build public confidence in the application of the new science."[10] Among other duties,

---

[5] Mary Warnock, *A Question of Life: The Warnock Report on Human Fertilisation and Embryology* (Oxford, UK: Basil Blackwell, 1985), 73.

[6] Ibid., xiv.

[7] Ibid., 62–63.

[8] Ibid., 63.

[9] Ibid., 66–67.

[10] "Cloning Issues in Reproduction, Science and Medicine," A Consultation Document, Human Genetics Advisory Commission and Human Fertilisation & Embryology Authority (London: January 1998), 10–11, accessed May 2004, http://www.hfea.gov.uk/AboutHFEA/Consultations.

the HGAC would "report on issues arising from new developments in human genetics that can be expected to have wider social, ethical and/or economic consequences, for example in relation to public health, insurance, patents and employment."[11] Perhaps it should not come as a surprise that the HFEA and the HGAC joined forces in 1998 to offer a consultation paper in response to the cloning of Dolly. The two groups formed the HGAC/HFEA Cloning Working Group and made clear that they would not license what they termed "reproductive cloning." That is, they would not endorse the production of identical human fetuses or babies through cloning. But they would endorse "other scientific and medical applications of nuclear replacement technology."[12]

C. Ben Mitchell (CBM): This is a helpful reminder that science develops over time and that once an idea like "test-tube babies" becomes normalized, other developments often seem less dramatic. Nigel Cameron, head of the Center for Policy on Emerging Technologies, calls this process "gradualism."[13] Gradualism is a bit like the proverbial frog in the kettle. If placed in a tea kettle of scalding water, a frog would leap immediately to safety. If, however, the frog were placed in tepid water, it would float happily to its death if the temperature of the kettle was rising only gradually. Science has its revolutions, but more often than not it evolves slowly over time. Gradualism explains why we do not always perceive the significance of single discoveries such as in vitro fertilization.

What is the different between what is called "reproductive cloning" and "therapeutic cloning"?

DJR: A diagram (with cellular components greatly magnified in their representation) may be helpful in understanding the difference.

Normal sexual reproduction is shown at the top left of the diagram; cloning is depicted at the top right. The result of the process is the generation of human embryos (zygotes), which are called blastocysts at the five- to seven-day stage. The blastocyst can be

[11] Ibid.

[12] Ibid.

[13] Nigel M. de S. Cameron, ed., *Embryos and Ethics* (Edinburgh: Rutherford House, 1987), 3.

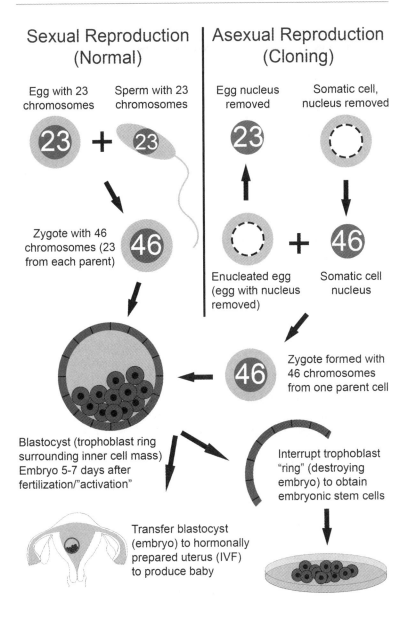

Sexual Reproduction (Normal)

Egg with 23 chromosomes   Sperm with 23 chromosomes

Zygote with 46 chromosomes (23 from each parent)

Blastocyst (trophoblast ring surrounding inner cell mass) Embryo 5-7 days after fertilization/"activation"

Transfer blastocyst (embryo) to hormonally prepared uterus (IVF) to produce baby

Asexual Reproduction (Cloning)

Egg nucleus removed   Somatic cell, nucleus removed

Enucleated egg (egg with nucleus removed)   Somatic cell nucleus

Zygote formed with 46 chromosomes from one parent cell

Interrupt trophoblast "ring" (destroying embryo) to obtain embryonic stem cells

transferred to a hormonally prepared uterus for gestation or can be used to produce stem cells. When stemcells are produced, the blastocyst is interrupted (thereby destroying the embryo), and the inner cell mass—these are the embryonic stem cells—is "harvested." What separates "reproductive" cloning (lower left) from "therapeutic" cloning (lower right) is the intent for the *use* of the *product*. In reproductive cloning the intended use of the embryo is a take-home cloned baby, a baby that has the same forty-six chromosomes as the donor of the somatic cell. In therapeutic cloning the intended use of the embryos is to procure embryonic stem cells to use in research that will (hopefully) lead to treatments or cures for other humans.

For the HGAC and the HFEA, a cloned baby was anathema, but using embryonic stem cells from cloned embryos was desirable, even if isolating those cells resulted in the death of the embryo. Because the term *cloning* was perceived so negatively, the Cloning Working Group referred to "therapeutic cloning" as cell nucleus replacement (CNR). In the United States it was typically called somatic cell nuclear transfer (SCNT). By whatever name, the process was that of cloning—the same technique that brought Dolly the sheep into the world.

Between 1991 and 1998, there were some 48,000 "spare" embryos and 118 created embryos used for research in Britain, according to the Donaldson Report.[14] During a similar period (1991–99), a total of 237,600 "unused" embryos had been destroyed.[15] It is little wonder that the Donaldson Report recommended the pursuit of CNR research for the purpose of understanding and developing treatment for mitochondrial diseases. The UK Human Reproductive Cloning Act of 2001 made it a crime "to place in a woman a human embryo that has been created by a method other than by fertilization."[16] By 2004, Britain had its first embryo stem cell bank and had issued its first license for the production of cloned embryos for stem cells. Therapeutic cloning was

---

[14] *Stem Cell Research: Medical Progress with Responsibility*, A Report from the Chief Medical Officer's Expert Group Reviewing the Potential of Developments in Stem Cell Research and Cell Nuclear Replacement to Benefit Human Health (London: Department of Health, June 2000), 5.

[15] "Briefing Note for Members of Parliament: Proposed Changes to the 1990 Human Fertilization and Embryology Act" (London: Wellcome Trust), Question 3.

[16] Explanatory Notes to Human Reproductive Cloning Act, 2001, c. 23.

seen as not only the way forward but also "a signal of (British) society's compassion and concern for those threatened by disease."[17]

CBM: Seeing how the language of compassion has shaped the public debates on cloning is revealing. Those who favor using embryos for research purposes are typically viewed as the compassionate ones. Embryonic stem cells have been described as nothing less than the equivalent of the elixir of life. Some scientists claim these cells can cure nearly every disease of the body, including many forms of cancer, Parkinson's disease, and dementia. The moral problem is, of course, that one must kill the embryo in order to isolate and extract the stem cells. If one believes human beings, even at the embryonic stage, are made in God's image, worthy of respect, and should not be unnecessarily harmed, then killing them to obtain stem cells is unethical. Destroying those embryos shows little compassion for unborn human beings.

Compounding the problem is the fact that the embryos are created outside of a woman's body. They will not be able to develop to their full maturity in vitro. Nevertheless, they are fully human, fully alive; and to justify killing them for their stem cells because they are not inside a uterus is to make protectable human life depend on geography: if an embryo is in a mother's body, it is protectable; if it is not in a womb, it is not protectable. This is ludicrous. Human embryos belong in human uteri. Living human beings, no matter how young and no matter where they are located, should be protected and allowed to mature.

DJR: Agreed. To make matters even more complex, international issues are at stake. Although the United Kingdom was the first to clone a mammal, it is not the only nation with cloning interests. On March 8, 2005, the UN General Assembly passed a declaration banning cloning in all its forms. A declaration of the UN differs from a convention in that the former is nonbinding and does not have the force of law. The UN cloning ban included "cloning for medical treatment," on the basis that cloning is "incompatible with human dignity and the protection of human life." Even though the ban was a nonbinding declaration, the vote was far from

---

[17] Michael Lawton, "Britain Approves Human Cloning," *Deutsche Welle*, August 12, 2004, 1, accessed August 19, 2004, http://www.dw-world.de/english/0,3367,144 6_A_1296131,00.html.

unanimous. Eighty-four nations voted in favor, 34 against; there were 37 abstentions, and 36 nations were absent. The United States voted for the declaration while Britain voted against it. Britain was joined in their vote against the ban by France, India, and the Russian Federation, all of whom wished to keep their "therapeutic" cloning options open. "The British delegate, who voted against, said the Assembly had missed an opportunity to adopt a convention prohibiting reproductive cloning because of the intransigence of those who failed to recognize that other sovereign States might want to permit strictly controlled applications of therapeutic cloning."[18]

"Therapeutic cloning," as it turns out, has been anything but strictly controlled. While no federal US law currently forbids cloning, a number of states have enacted various laws. The state of California was the first to ban reproductive cloning in 1997 but allows "cloning for research."[19] In early 2004, then New Jersey Governor McGreevey signed into law a bill that purportedly outlawed cloning. The provisions included:

> A person who knowingly engages or assists, directly or indirectly, in the cloning of a human being is guilty of a crime of the first degree.
>
> As used in this section, "cloning of a human being" means the replication of a human individual by cultivating a cell with genetic material through the egg, embryo, fetal and newborn stages into a new human individual.[20]

The law in New Jersey is not an anticloning law at all, however. What is prohibited is the birth of a cloned human. Cloned human embryos, if/when they are produced, can be mined for their stem cells with the state's blessing.

Now the feat of garnering embryonic stem cells from cloned embryos seems to have been accomplished in Oregon with the announcement by Mitalipov and his colleagues. As with any new

---

[18] "General Assembly approves declaration banning all forms of cloning," *UN News Centre*, March 8, 2005, accessed May 31, 2013, http://www.un.org/apps/news/story.asp?NewsID=13576&Cr=cloning&Cr1.

[19] "Human Cloning Laws," NCSL, West Group, National Conference of State Legislatures, updated January 2008, accessed June 18, 2013, http://www.ncsl.org/issues-research/health/human-cloning-laws.aspx.

[20] New Jersey P.L. 2003, C. 203 (approved January 2, 2004), accessed June 18, 2013, http://www.njleg.state.nj.us/2002/Bills/AL03/203_.HTM.

research, replication of the work will be needed for verification of the results. Of course, that means more cloned embryos will be destroyed for their embryonic stem cells.

CBM: Although some states prohibit or regulate various types of cloning, I think few people realize no federal law in the United States forbids the cloning of a human being. Currently, there are restrictions on the use of federal funds for research that ends in the destruction of human embryos, but those do not apply to the use of private funds. It is shocking that almost two decades after Dolly we have not been able to reach a public-policy consensus on something like cloning a human being.

DJR: It *is* shocking. But the British experience is a reminder that there are many stakeholders in the debate. The more stakeholders, typically the more difficult it is to frame effective policy. And, to be fair, the science is developing so rapidly that making policies that will last is an increasingly difficult proposition.

In November 2006, two British research teams applied to the HFEA for licenses "to derive stem cells from human embryos." But there was a problem. Too few human eggs were available to sustain the research. So the investigators proposed "using animal eggs, from which they had removed almost all the animal genetic material (DNA). These embryos would be a kind of hybrid, known as a cytoplasmic hybrid embryo."[21] The HFEA held a consultation in September 2007 and "agreed on a policy for the licensing of cytoplasmic hybrid research."[22]

CBM: The image of animal-human hybrids goes back to ancient Greek mythology. "Chimeras" (Kai-MAIR-uhz) in Homer's *Iliad* were composed of three animals: a lion, a snake, and a goat. The distinguished magazine *National Geographic* used the term to describe an experiment in 2003, in which Chinese scientists at the Shanghai Second Medical University successfully fused human cells with rabbit eggs. These were called chimeric organisms. Properly,

---

[21] Human Fertilisation and Embryology Authority, "Review of Hybrids and Chimeras," accessed June 19, 2013, http://www.hfea.gov.uk/519.html.

[22] Ibid.

though, *chimera* refers to the combining of "cells from two genetically different individuals."[23]

Human-animal hybrids are created by combining human gametes (sperm and egg) with animal gametes. According to the UK's *Daily Mail*, as of 2011, more than 150 human-animal hybrid embryos were created in British laboratories since the Human Fertilisation and Embryology Act of 2008, which called for regulation of human-animal hybrid research.[24]

Human-animal hybrid research raises troubling questions. For instance, what is the moral status of an embryo created using a rabbit egg and a human nucleus (a cybrid)? Is it animal or is it human? How much human DNA is required for us to recognize a new organism as human? Or is the organism a novel species? Do they fall under human rights protection, or should we only worry about giving them the same ethical consideration as animals in research?

DJR: These are profound questions. And other crucial questions arise as a result of these types of laboratory manipulations. For example, using these techniques could allow a child to have three or more parents. Take a human egg from one female and remove its nucleus. Replace that nucleus with the nucleus of a different woman's egg. Then, using sperm from the husband or a donor, fertilize the egg and transfer it to a uterus. A resulting baby would have three parents.

Embryos with three parents are being created to avoid mitochondrial diseases. In the UK, mitochondrial diseases afflict approximately 100 children per year. Mitochondria, the energy source for cells, possess their own DNA. That DNA includes thirty-seven genes, of which thirteen seem to be of greatest interest. Since mitochondria are only passed down from mother to child, scientists have seized on this idea of replacing the faulty mitochondrial DNA of the mother with the nonaffected mitochondrial DNA of an egg donor. The resulting child would have the chromosomes (nuclear DNA) of his/her mother and father and the mitochondrial DNA

[23] Andrea L. Bonnicksen, *Chimeras, Hybrids and Interspecies Research: Politics and Policymaking* (Washington, DC: Georgetown University Press, 2009), 10.

[24] Daniel Martin and Simon Caldwell, "150 Human Animal Hybrids Grown in UK Labs; Embryos Have Been Produced Secretively for the Past Three Years," *The Daily Mail*, July 22, 2011, accessed June 18, 2013, http://www.dailymail.co.uk/sciencetech/article-2017818/Embryos-involving-genes-animals-mixed-humans-produced-secretively-past-years.html.

of the egg donor. The Nuffield Council on Bioethics has, after some study, declared this "ethical." According to the BBC, Dr. Geoff Watts, who led the inquiry, said: "If further research shows these techniques to be sufficiently safe and effective, we think it would be ethical for families to use them if they wished to, provided they receive an appropriate level of information and support."[25]

Several questions have been raised about the three-parent embryo. One is, will the egg donor be a parent to the child? According to the HFEA, the answer is no. Dr. David King, director of Human Genetics Alert, voiced his concerns:

> Just as Frankenstein's creation was produced by sticking together bits from different bodies, it seems that there is no grotesquerie, no violation of the norms of nature or human culture at which scientists and their bioethical helpers will balk.
>
> The proposed techniques are both unnecessary, and highly dangerous in the medium term, since they set a precedent for allowing the creation of genetically modified designer babies.[26]

He argued that such techniques would affect many generations and crossed "what is normally considered the most important ethical line in the prevention of a new eugenics," and this was "precisely how slippery slopes get created."[27]

CBM: I understand exactly what he means. The technology might be used at first as a "treatment" for mitochondrial diseases, but in an age where personal autonomy and desire satisfaction trump all other values, there seems to be no reason the technology will not eventually be used simply because three individuals *want* to have a child together. And why stop at three? An egg could come from one woman, a nucleus from another person, and sperm from a male. Then the embryo could be transferred to yet another woman's uterus. And I'm sure there will be countless additional ways in the future to combine DNA to generate "designer children." The

---

[25] James Gallagher, "Three-Person IVF 'Is Ethical' to Treat Mitochondrial Disease," *BBC NEWS*, June 11, 2012, accessed June 18, 2013, http://www.bbc.co.uk/news/health-18393682.

[26] Ibid.

[27] Ibid.

1997 movie *Gattaca* turns out to have been prescient. Science fiction often becomes science fact.

If I understand correctly, embryo experimentation—never mind treatments using embryonic stem cells—will require a large number of human eggs. Where will researchers get these eggs?

DJR: Currently, females of reproductive age are targeted as the providers of eggs for research. Women are usually compensated for egg "donation" for fertility treatments in the United States, but compensation for eggs donated for research is not the norm. Massachusetts and California have laws in place prohibiting such payments, although how long those laws will be in place is unclear. In 2008, it was reported that after advertising for two years and spending $100,000, a Harvard lab finally secured one egg donor for its research.[28] Proposition 71, which formed the California Institute of Regenerative Medicine (CIRM) in 2004, also dictated that there would be no reimbursement to women for egg donation beyond direct costs. A 2006 law extended that prohibition to all research in California. Time will tell whether those prohibitions stand.

Why were prohibitions of egg "donation" compensation put in place? Was it concern that women who donate eggs were put at unnecessary risk by the procedure? Some risks of egg donation arise from the hormones injected and include ovarian hyperstimulation syndrome (OHSS), which in extreme form, can cause kidney failure or death. These occurrences are rare, notably.[29] Other risks are posed by the procedure to "harvest" or procure the eggs, which involves anesthesia and a minor surgical procedure. Whether the hormonal stimulation and egg donation will result in decreased fertility of the donors is yet to be seen. A government-sponsored workshop convened to assess the risks of egg donation for stem cell research addressed concerns regarding the possibility of increased cancer rates in egg donors:

---

[28] Brendan Maher, "Egg Shortage Hits Race to Clone Human Stem Cells," *Nature* 453 (2008), 828–29, published online June 11, 2008, accessed June 19, 2013, http://www.nature.com/news/2008/080611/full/453828a.html.

[29] Linda Giudice, Eileen Santa, and Robert Pool, eds., "Assessing the Medical Risks of Human Oocyte Donation for Stem Cell Research: Workshop Report," Institute of Medicine and National Research Council (Washington, DC: National Academies Press, 2007), 29, accessed June 19, 2013, http://books.nap.edu/openbook.php?record_id=11832&page=29.

Many observers have worried that the use of fertility drugs could lead to an increased risk of cancer—in particular, breast, ovarian, and uterine (including endometrial) cancers. One must be careful in interpreting epidemiological studies of women taking fertility drugs, because all of these cancers are more common in women with infertility, so merely comparing women taking fertility drugs with women in the general population inevitably shows an increased cancer risk. When the analysis is done correctly, accounting for the increased cancer risk due to infertility, the evidence does not support a relationship between fertility drugs and an increased prevalence of breast or ovarian cancer. More research is required to examine what the long-term impact fertility drugs may be on breast and ovarian cancer prevalence rates. For uterine cancer, the numbers are too small to achieve statistical significance, but it is at least possible that fertility drugs may indeed cause some increased risk of uterine cancer.[30]

CBM: So the risks to egg donors are not necessarily known currently. Is this why there was a prohibition of compensating women for yielding up their eggs for stem cell research?

DJR: Not really. The US National Academy of Sciences (NAS) guidelines barring compensation were set in part to protect poor people from being exploited by labs that might offer large sums of money, along the lines of rules barring compensation for organ donation. But Alta Charo, a lawyer and bioethicist at the University of Wisconsin Law School in Madison, who liaised with the NAS committee that set donor-compensation guidelines in 2005, says the move was as much political as ethical. In California supporters of Proposition 71, which allows funding for stem-cell and cloning research in the absence of federal funding, adopted compensation prohibition in part, Charo claims, "to assuage a fringe group of the women's movement" that was aligned against the assisted-reproduction community.[31]

---

[30] Ibid.
[31] Maher, "Egg Shortage Hits Race to Clone Human Stem Cells."

That prohibition of compensation may be short-lived, however. The competition for embryonic stem cell lines continues, and as the case at the beginning of this chapter indicates, new claims have been staked by the Oregon group. That group was unhindered by rules that forbid compensating females for their eggs, for there is no such law in Oregon. The women whose eggs were used in the OHSU study were each paid $3,000–$7,000.[32]

Conclusion

The temptation to manipulate another human life is almost irresistible in an age of scientism. Despite efforts to prohibit the birth of a human clone (or perhaps later, a human-animal hybrid), we likely will have to face these questions in the not too distant future. Someone, somewhere, will probably do it. Perhaps they already have.

Yet our culture is exquisitely ill equipped morally to deal with the reality of a human clone in our midst. The clone would first have to suffer the notoriety of being born through human somatic cell nuclear transfer. Next, his or her future would be shaped by someone else's past. That is to say, those who rear the clone will, no doubt, want to duplicate the environment of the donor as much as possible so the clone would be everything the parents desired the new person to be. If parents want another Jane Doe, they will have to reproduce as much as possible the environment in which the young Jane grew up. And they will want to teach Jane 2 to walk and talk like Jane 1. Whether or not it works, it does not bode well for human freedom.

Furthermore, proprietary interests may take over. Who owns a clone—the cloned, the clone, or the cloner? In the commodified world of biotechnology, the one with the most investment money is likely to win. Or perhaps the one who owns the patent will have ownership. Thus, prospective parents might be able to purchase a clone, or someone might be able to license the technology, but the market will determine the asking price. Will the price be set in pounds, dollars, Euros, or yen? Remember, the market is global.

---

[32] Charlotte Schubert, "California Bill Poised to Lift Restrictions on Egg Donation," *Nature News*, June 18, 2013, accessed June 19, 2013, http://www.nature.com/news/california-bill-poised-to-lift-restrictions-on-egg-donation-1.13218.

In our view all human cloning should be forthrightly banned. No human-animal hybrid embryos should be produced. Just because science can clone human beings or create human-animal hybrids doesn't mean scientists should do so. We are not technological determinists. Some things just should not be done.

"I was convinced that there was still plenty of time." With those haunting words, Aldous Huxley looked back to the 1931 publication of his prophetic book, *Brave New World*. Huxley's vision of an oppressive culture of authoritarian control and social engineering was among the more shocking literary events of the twentieth century. But a mere twenty-seven years after the publication of his novel, Huxley was already aware that he had sorely underestimated the threat of modern technocratic society. A technological threat to our culture and our humanity looms over us today in the form of human cloning and hybrid research.

Additional Resources

Heimbach, Daniel R. "Cloning Humans: Dangerous, Unjustifiable, and Genuinely Immoral." *Valpariso University Law Review* 32, no. 2 (Spring 1998): 1–4.

Kass, Leon R., and James Q. Wilson. *The Ethics of Human Cloning.* Washington, DC: The AEI Press, Publisher for the American Enterprise Institute, 1998.

Klotzko, Arlene Judith, ed. *The Cloning Sourcebook.* Oxford: Oxford University Press, 2001.

The President's Council on Bioethics. *Human Cloning and Human Dignity: An Ethical Inquiry.* Washington, DC: The President's Council on Bioethics, 2002.

Part IV

Remaking/Faking Life

Chapter 8

Aging and Life-Extension Technologies

Case: *"Immortal Avatar: Russian Project Seeks to Create Robot with Human Brain"*[1]

What do you get when you cross James Cameron's idea, Robert White's work with chimps, and the deep pockets of Russian Dmitry Itskov? Something called the Russian 2045 Movement, which is a robot that closely resembles a human from far away and close-up and contains a human brain and personality. This is not a joke. According to the company's website, the project consists of four stages:

Stage 1—called **Avatar**—is aimed at creating a robotic copy of the human body, controlled through a brain-computer interface. This stage is to be completed by 2020.

Stage 2—**Body B**—to create an Avatar in which a human brain is transplanted at the end of one's life. This stage is to be completed by 2025.

---

[1] "Immortal Avatar: Russian Project Seeks to Create Robot with Human Brain," *RT*, April 30, 2012, accessed June 13, 2013, http://rt.com/news/prime-time/avatar -russian-scientists-brain-983.

Stage 3—Re-brain—to create an Avatar with an artificial brain, in which a human personality or consciousness is transferred at the end of one's life. This stage is to start in 2030 and to be completed by 2035.

Stage 4—Hologram-like body—A hologram-like avatar. To be started in 2040 and completed by 2045.[2]

The goal? A new generation of android robots: able to think for themselves, as well as immortal. Itskov describes the avatar as "a way to combat nature." While that may be the distant goal, there has been some practical application in the near term:

> Not all of the projects being developed in Zelenograd sound like they've come straight out of a sci-fi movie. Some, like the robotic hand of the prototype, are actually being used to help people who have lost limbs.
>
> So far, the hands operate separately from the head and the body, though the work on them is still in progress. Pneumatic muscles clench the fingers into a fist; compressed air forces them to contract.
>
> "This definitely can be used to help disabled people. We already ran some experiments—a subject without a hand tried this technology. He said the hand worked for him. All it takes is to attach electrodes to the undamaged part of the arm so they can read the muscle activity," software engineer Andrey Telezhinsky explained to RT.[3]

Discussion

C. Ben Mitchell (CBM): Do you want to live forever? Some will answer a resounding "No!" and others will reply, "Yes, but what's the catch?" The dream of escaping death and living forever has been around a long time. It is the promise of the great religions and the stuff of ancient fables and myths like the Fountain of Youth. The vision of immortality has never been more vivid than today.

---

[2] Ibid. (emphasis added).
[3] Ibid.

In his turn-of-the-millennium volume *Immortality: How Science Is Extending Your Life Span and Changing the World*, Ben Bova, MD, claims that

> physical immortality is within sight . . . The first immortal human beings are probably living among us today. You might be one of them. There are men and women who may be able to live for centuries, perhaps even extend their life spans indefinitely. For them, death will not be inevitable.[4]

How could that be possible? How could humans achieve immortality? The answer is technology. In fact, life extension—along with the quack medicines and slick magazines promising it—has become a huge industry. We are promised that nutritional supplements and snake oils will free us from this mortal coil.

At the same time, this quest has a serious side. After all, historically, we have made huge strides in extending human life, haven't we?

D. Joy Riley (DJR): To be sure. The American historian William McNeill says that about 500 BC pathogens (germs) began to impact Asian and European civilizations, causing diphtheria, smallpox, and influenza among other maladies.[5] These pathogens flourished in cities and during invasions, as people carrying differing pathogens and differing immunities came into close contact with one another. Thucydides described one epidemic that spread from Africa to Persia and reached Greece by 430 BC, soon after the Peloponnesian War began. The Athenians lost a quarter of their forces, and over the next four years, an equal portion of Greece's population died as well.[6]

In addition to these diseases, epidemics of plague, dysentery, measles, and syphilis (to name a few more) decimated entire populations. Describing the cities of Spain and Portugal at the time of great exploration, Kenneth F. Kiple writes:

---

[4] Ben Bova, *Immortality: How Science Is Extending Your Life Span—and Changing the World* (San Francisco: Harper Perennial, 2000), xiii.

[5] Kenneth F. Kiple, "The History of Disease," in *The Cambridge Illustrated History of Medicine*, ed. Roy Porter (Cambridge, UK: Cambridge University Press, 1996; repr., 2000; first paperback edition, 2001), 24.

[6] Ibid., 25.

Bathing was frowned upon, and clothing was coarse and changed infrequently. Hence the human body was a veritable nest of lice and fleas. Human wastes were flung into the streets to mingle with those of dogs and horses. All of this was paradise for flies that flitted from faeces to food. Water for drinking and cooking was practically a soup of microorganisms.[7]

In addition to infectious diseases, nutritional deficiencies—particularly of protein but also vitamins—shortened lives over the centuries. Over the last 100 plus years, though, longevity has increased. This is true particularly in the United States, but we are not alone.

Gains in longevity were fastest in the first half of the 20th century. These advances were largely attributed to "an enormous scientific breakthrough—the germ theory of disease" which led to the eradication and control of numerous infectious and parasitic diseases, especially among infants and children.[8] . . . The new theory led to an entirely new approach to preventative medicine, practiced both by departments of public health and by individuals. Interventions included boiling bottles and milk, washing hands, protecting food from flies, isolating sick children, ventilating rooms, and improving water supply and sewage disposal. Beginning in the 1940s, the control of infectious diseases was also aided by the increasing distribution and usage of antibiotics, including penicillin and sulfa drugs.[9]

Although improvements in hygiene and the invention of penicillin in the early part of the century cannot be overstated, from the mid-twentieth century onward, increasing control of cardiovascular and cerebrovascular diseases is credited with increasing life expectancy in the US.[10]

---

[7] Ibid., 29–30.

[8] S. H. Preston and M. Haines, *Fatal Years: Child Mortality in Late Nineteenth Century America*, National Bureau of Economic Research, Series on Long-Term Factors in Economic Development (Princeton, NJ: Princeton University Press, 1991). Quoted in Laura B. Shrestha, *Life Expectancy in the United States* (Congressional Research Service, Library of Congress, updated August 16, 2006), 6, accessed June 22, 2013, http://www.aging.senate .gov/crs/aging1.pdf.

[9] Ibid., 6–7.

[10] Ibid., 7.

Here is a graph of life expectancy at birth for the US, from 1900 to 2009.[11] Note the impact of the influenza epidemic of 1918.

CBM: These improvements have had remarkable results. In 2008, it was estimated that there were 506 million people aged sixty-five years and older in the world.[12] By 2040 there will be 1.3 billion people sixty-five and older.[13]

A major demographic shift is about to take place in the US. According to the National Academies' report *Aging and the Macroeconomy: Long-Term Implications of an Older Population*, the ratio of adults aged sixty-five and over, compared with people aged

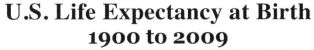

---

[11] From Dr. Miguel A. Faria, "Medical History—Hygiene and Sanitation," *Medical Sentinel* 2002; 7(4): 122–23, accessed December 7, 2013, http://www.haciendapub.com/medicalsentinel/medical-history-hygiene-and-sanitation. Used by permission.

[12] Kevin Kinsella and Wan He, International Programs Center, Population Division, United States Census Bureau, "Unprecedented Global Aging Examined in New Census Bureau Report Commissioned by the National Institute on Aging," Press Release July 20, 2009, accessed June 22, 2013, http://www.census.gov/newsroom/releases/archives/aging_population/cb09-108.html.

[13] Ibid.

twenty to sixty-four, will increase by 80 percent in the coming decades. This shift is happening for two reasons. First, people are living longer. The average life expectancy has risen from forty-seven years in 1900 to seventy-eight years today and is projected to be 84.5 years by the year 2050. Second, many couples are choosing to have fewer children and to have those children somewhat later in life.

As remarkable as this might seem, for some people these advances both in life expectancy and life span are too slow and intermittent. They want to see life span increased indefinitely and the sooner the better.

DJR: Yes, in fact, an entire philosophical school has developed around the promise of life extension: the transhumanist movement. The World Transhumanist Association (WTA) was founded in 1998, by Oxford philosophers Nick Bostrom and David Pearce. The WTA claims that the human species is in transition, hence the "trans" in transhumanism. The aim of the WTA is to do something to propel that transition. Its tagline is: "For the ethical use of technology to extend human capabilities." The Transhumanist Declaration states, in part:

- Humanity will be radically changed by technology in the future. We foresee the feasibility of redesigning the human condition, including such parameters as the inevitability of aging, limitations on human and artificial intellects, unchosen psychology, suffering, and our confinement to the planet earth.
- Transhumanists advocate the moral right for those who so wish to use technology to extend their mental and physical (including reproductive) capacities and to improve their control over their own lives. We seek personal growth beyond our current biological limitations.
- Transhumanism advocates the well-being of all sentience (whether in artificial intellects, humans, posthumans, or non-human animals) and encompasses many principles of modern humanism.[14]

---

[14] See "Transhumanist Declaration," accessed March 18, 2014, http://humanityplus.org /philosophy/transhumanist-declaration.

In other words, instead of redesigning the environment of human beings (as with the twentieth-century revolution), human beings themselves will be redesigned. The movement has declared war on aging and every other human limitation.

CBM: The movement is gaining followers, some of them well connected. For instance, Ray Kurzweil is an American philanthropist, author, and award-winning inventor. He is responsible for several devices that help the hearing impaired and is the inventor of the Kurzweil musical keyboard.

Kurzweil's quest for life extension is personal. His father died at age fifty-eight from heart disease. When Kurzweil realized his own cholesterol and other cardiac indicators were abnormal, he took action. He now claims he has slowed his aging and corrected all the risk factors he can. How? Says Kurzweil, "I take 250 supplements (pills) a day and receive a half-dozen intravenous therapies each week (basically nutritional supplements delivered into my bloodstream, thereby bypassing my GI tract)."

His 650-page magnum opus, *The Singularity Is Near*, is filled with scientific data and suffused with the enthusiasm of a new convert. Kurzweil's subtitle gives a clue to the thesis of the book, *When Humans Transcend Biology*. A futurist and aspiring immortalist, Kurzweil argues that humanity will reach "the Singularity" in 2045. The Singularity is that "future period representing the culmination of the merger of our biological thinking and existence with our technology, resulting in a world that is still human but that transcends our biological roots."[15]

In an article he wrote for the British newspaper *The Sun*, Kurzweil claimed:

> I and many other scientists now believe that in around 20 years we will have the means to reprogramme our bodies' stone-age software so we can halt, then reverse, ageing. Then nanotechnology will let us live forever. Ultimately, nanobots will replace blood cells and do their work thousands of times more effectively. Within 25 years we will be able to do an Olympic sprint for 15 minutes without taking a breath, or go scuba-diving for four hours without

---

[15] Ray Kurzweil, *The Singularity Is Near: When Humans Transcend Biology* (New York: Penguin, 2006), 9, 136.

oxygen. Heart-attack victims—who haven't taken advan-
tage of widely available bionic hearts—will calmly drive
to the doctors for a minor operation as their blood bots
keep them alive. Nanotechnology will extend our mental
capacities to such an extent we will be able to write books
within minutes. If we want to go into virtual-reality mode,
nanobots will shut down brain signals and take us wherever we want to go. Virtual sex will become commonplace.
And in our daily lives, hologram like figures will pop in
our brain to explain what is happening. So we can look
forward to a world where humans become cyborgs, with
artificial limbs and organs.[16]

Yet one must wonder what this cyborg world would look like.
Kurzweil plans to find out. Now in his mid-sixties, Kurzweil hopes
to stay alive long enough to achieve physical immortality when the
Singularity arrives.

Though he rightly may be called eccentric, Kurzweil is no crack-
pot. He has been called the "the rightful heir to Thomas Edison"
and was selected as one of the top entrepreneurs in America by
Inc. magazine. Moreover, Kurzweil is one of a growing number
of people who call themselves transhumanists. Each year he hosts
a Singularity Summit, a multiday conference that brings together
scientists, inventors, philosophers, and others to "explore areas
such as biotechnology & bioinformatics, energy & environmental
systems, networks & computing systems, AI & robotics, medicine
& neuroscience, and nanotechnology."[17]

Another important figure in the movement is Aubrey de Grey.
Based in Cambridge, England, de Grey calls himself a biogeron-
tologist. He points out in a recent book, *Ending Aging*, that around
150,000 people die each day worldwide. Of those, he asserts, "about
two-thirds die of aging." De Grey laments that these numbers do
not galvanize us to action the way other human tragedies do. We
have been lulled to sleep, he says, by notions like "natural death"
when there is nothing natural about dying of aging. Thus, de Grey
has devised a SENS program to combat our mortality. "Strategies

[16] Cited in Amy Willis, "Immortality Only 20 Years Away Says Scientist," *The Telegraph*,
September 22, 2009, accessed June 22, 2013, http://www.telegraph.co.uk/science/science
-news/6217676/Immortality-only-20-years-away-says-scientist.html.
[17] "Singularity Summit," accessed June 27, 2013, http://singularitysummit.com.

for Engineered Negligible Senescence" include a number of potential therapies aimed at eliminating aging.[18]

Winsome and somewhat eccentric, Aubrey de Grey is one of the cofounders of the Methuselah Foundation. The foundation sponsors, among other things, the Mprize, a monetary prize awarded to anyone who finds an efficient way to rejuvenate or significantly extend the life span of mice. Why mice? Because the so-called mouse model is one of the best tools leading to research on humans. That is why we hear so much in the news media about scientific developments using mice as research subjects.

What are we to make of these audacious claims? How should we think about transhumanism and life extension?

DJR: Their voices are not the only ones we should consider. Although there are, and will increasingly be, ways we can extend human life span, Jay Olshansky, a senior longevity researcher at the University of Illinois in Chicago, maintains that the science demonstrates that however much we would like to extend our life spans, there are built-in limits. In his book *The Quest for Immortality*, Olshansky maintains that senescence, the death of cells, is a fact of life. We have already extended life to its far limits. Some cancers, Alzheimer's, and other age-related illnesses are evidences that we have pushed the biological boundaries. Extending life would not eliminate these diseases. He also warns that legitimate science repudiates the pseudoscience behind hyped-up claims that longevity can be achieved through the use of melatonin, DHEA, and extreme forms of alternative medicine. We would be better off, says Olshansky, getting plenty of exercise and enjoying a more relaxed lifestyle. The Fountain of Youth remains as elusive as ever.[19]

CBM: Transhumanists are not only interested in extending the life of the body; they are also interested in escaping the body. Transhumanists do not identify aging as the only problem we face. Human beings are finite and limited. In addition to limited life spans, we have limited IQs and memories. We are limited by time and space. We have emotional and spiritual limitations. So,

---

[18] Aubrey de Grey, *Ending Aging: The Rejuvenation Breakthroughs That Could Reverse Human Aging in Our Lifetime* (New York: St. Martin's Griffin, 2008), 8.

[19] Bruce A. Carnes and S. Jay Olshansky, *The Quest for Immortality: Science at the Frontiers of Aging* (New York: W. W. Norton, 2002).

they ask, why not find ways to transfer human consciousness into machines? Think cyborgs. Or why not live in some vast neural network like the Internet? Think *The Matrix*. Why stay tethered to these carbon-based, aging bodies anyhow?

No one knows to what degree emerging biotechnologies like nanotechnology, genetic engineering, robotics, and artificial intelligence will allow us to live longer. But the impetus behind the immortality movement raises some profound questions.

As a physician, how do you think about aging?

DJR: Like much of life, aging has it benefits and liabilities. I had the privilege of growing up in the midst of extended family so I saw older people up close. Being trained as an internist, I have seen many older people as patients. That was particularly true when I worked in a nursing home. Some of those patients had been prisoners in the concentration camps of WWII. Reading stories about the Holocaust teaches me in some ways; having a patient with a number tattooed on the inside of her left wrist teaches me about the Holocaust in a totally different way. At our holiday table last December, we had four octogenarians as our dinner guests. Although from different continents, all had lived through a major war and had experienced eighty plus years in the world. That dinner was an encounter with "living history." "When an elderly person dies, a library burns"—so goes an African proverb that has stuck with me for a number of years. That has the ring of truth to it.

Even so, "aging is not for wimps," my husband and I remind each other. There are difficulties and unpleasantness aplenty. Friends complain of spending their retirement visiting the doctor's office. Knees and hips wear out, and energy can be exhausted long before the to-do list is completed. Family members and friends leave this life and our circle before we are ready, perhaps, and sometimes after significant suffering. Medicine can often help, either through curative means or interventions that improve conditions, at least for a while. Eventually, though, bodies (and sometimes, minds) fail.

What do I think about that? I think it is painful and sad at times; yet there is a rightness to it, as well. It teaches us several things:

1. We are not all there is. At some point others will touch the things we have fingered and claim ownership of them.

Therefore, we need to hold things (possessions) lightly but people in high regard.

2. Wisdom counts. It is the rare centenarian who is admired for bodily beauty, but a goodly number of them are admired for their wisdom. Therefore, we should spend our time getting wisdom. Exercise is good, including of the mind. Getting wisdom, however, is more important.

3. We often die as we have lived, especially when "old and full of years." If we are selfish now, our families and friends (if we have any) should not expect to see a different person as we approach death. It has been my experience that if a person is cranky in his life, his experience surrounding death is not apt to be much different. By the same token, those who are delightful in life come to their death in much the same way as they have lived. One caveat is that those who are delightful in life are usually the ones who know that this life is not all there is to living and look forward to seeing their Maker. Hence, death is not unexpected.

Frankly, I am beginning to feel like an "elder" as I write this. Let's turn to wisdom. Theologically, how should we think about aging?

CBM: Aging begins at conception and continues throughout natural life. Aging is not a disease to be cured but a reality of the human condition to be celebrated. The sage author of Proverbs 16:31 has said, "Gray hair is a glorious crown; it is found in the way of righteousness." In our youth-idolizing age, we have turned this adage upside down. In the past youthfulness was something one "got over." Perpetual adolescence was viewed as a vice. Today the television and movie industries portray senior adults as either disabled or otherwise pitiable. Yet, from the biblical perspective, virtue and wisdom are the fruits of years of experience.

Furthermore, the gift of years is meant to provide us with additional opportunities to glorify God. Thus, the psalmist says: "Even when I am old and gray, God, do not abandon me. Then I proclaim Your power to another generation, Your strength to all who are to come" (Ps 71:18). The image of spiritual vitality even in old age is pictured vividly in Psalm 92:12–15: "The righteous thrive like a palm tree and grow like a cedar tree in Lebanon. Planted in the house of the LORD, they thrive in the courts of our God. They will still bear fruit in old age, healthy and green, to declare: 'The LORD is just; He is my rock, and there is no unrighteousness in Him.'

To be sure, aspects of aging make life difficult and challenging. Age-related illnesses, the death of loved ones and peers, and other burdens of life can tarnish our later years. But that need not be the case necessarily as the words of the apostle Paul remind us:

> Though our outer person is being destroyed, our inner person is being renewed day by day. For our momentary light affliction is producing for us an absolutely incomparable eternal weight of glory. So we do not focus on what is seen, but on what is unseen. For what is seen is temporary, but what is unseen is eternal.
>
> For we know that if our temporary, earthly dwelling is destroyed, we have a building from God, an eternal dwelling in the heavens, not made with hands. Indeed, we groan in this body, desiring to put on our dwelling from heaven, since, when we are clothed, we will not be found naked. Indeed, we groan while we are in this tent, burdened as we are, because we do not want to be unclothed but clothed, so that mortality may be swallowed up by life. And the One who prepared us for this very purpose is God, who gave us the Spirit as a down payment.
>
> So, we are always confident and know that while we are at home in the body we are away from the Lord. For we walk by faith, not by sight, and we are confident and satisfied to be out of the body and at home with the Lord. Therefore, whether we are at home or away, we make it our aim to be pleasing to Him. (2 Cor 4:16–5:9)

We do see the tension in Paul's experience. He longs to be with the Lord in his heavenly building, but he is also content in his earthly tent. In between there is groaning but not despair. There are troubles, but as long as the Spirit is present with us, we can endure until the end. Until then our aim, our goal, our desire is to please God.

DJR: It seems to me that these words of the apostle Paul address some of the issues raised by the transhumanists. What do you think?

CBM: Interestingly, the transhumanists and Christians seem to have some common concerns. We share:

- The quest for the good life
- Longing for immortality
- Pursuit of the relief of human suffering
- Appreciation for technology's benefits

Where we differ is in the means to achieve these aims. For Christians the good life and the goods of life are found in God and his presence in our lives. The good life is not defined by the number of years one lives but by the reality of God's presence in however many years one lives.

While we, like the apostle Paul, long for immortality, Christians understand that they already possess it. We are all immortal beings! We will live from conception through all of eternity. This is the salvation Paul celebrates in Romans 8:38–39 when he says, "For I am persuaded that not even death or life, angels or rulers, things present or things to come, hostile powers, height or depth, or any other created thing will have the power to separate us from the love of God that is in Christ Jesus our Lord!"

At the same time Christians should certainly be sensitive to the needs of those who are suffering. We lament age-related diseases and should do what we can to ameliorate the suffering of those who experience the pain and disability that is sometimes associated with those diseases. Technological advances may indeed be the vehicle for the relief of that suffering and pain. All things being equal, we should encourage and celebrate those advances. So long as they are ethically developed, treatments or cures for age-associated cardiovascular disease, cancer, arthritis, cataracts, osteoporosis, type 2 diabetes, hypertension, and Alzheimer's disease would be wonderful assets to the quality of life of an aging population.

Another place we differ with the transhumanists is in loathing every human limitation. Because we are creatures and not creators, we accept most limitations as gifts from the One who made us. We are not sovereign; we are finite. In fact, omniscience would be a terrible burden for a human to bear. To know all things without the power to alter them would be torture. Since we are aware, to quote Lord Acton, that "power corrupts and absolute power corrupts absolutely," we know that we could not bear the burden of omnipotence. Although it might be nice from time to time to be in more than one place, omnipresence is not for humans. We are located, embodied creatures.

So, say the transhumanists, we must give up our humanity—become posthuman. But for Christians that would only make matters worse. Our salvation was purchased by the God-man, Christ Jesus—fully God and fully human. His humanity was offered for our humanity. His resurrection is the guarantee of our resurrection. As Paul expresses the truth in his letter to the Corinthian church:

> But now Christ has been raised from the dead, the first-fruits of those who have fallen asleep. For since death came through a man, the resurrection of the dead also comes through a man. For as in Adam all die, so also in Christ all will be made alive. But each in his own order: Christ the firstfruits; afterward, at His coming, those who belong to Christ. (1 Cor 15:20–23)

Or as countless numbers of Christians confess each week through the Apostles' Creed, we believe in the life everlasting:

I believe in God, the Father almighty,
Creator of heaven and earth.
I believe in Jesus Christ, his only Son, our Lord,
who was conceived by the Holy Spirit,
born of the virgin Mary,
suffered under Pontius Pilate,
was crucified, died, and was buried;
he descended to the dead.
On the third day he rose again;
he ascended into heaven,
he is seated at the right hand of the Father,
and he will come to judge the living and the dead.
I believe in the Holy Spirit,
the holy catholic Church,
the communion of saints,
the forgiveness of sins,
the resurrection of the body,
and the life everlasting.
Amen.

Conclusion

Increasingly, Western culture—especially American culture—has come to loathe every facet of aging. Mushrooming interest in cosmetic surgery, obsessive consumption of antioxidants, and the technological quest for immortality are phenomena of a relatively affluent and increasingly ageist society.

We must resist both ageism and fatalism. Aging itself is not a disease to be conquered. Likewise, we do not have to accept stoically every limitation associated with aging. Navigating the space between these extremes requires faithful discipleship.

Additional Resources

Kurzweil, Ray. *The Singularity Is Near: When Humans Transcend Biology*. New York: Viking-Penguin, 2005.

Mitchell, C. Ben, Edmund D. Pellegrino, Jean Bethke Elshtain, John F. Kilner, and Scott B. Rae. *Biotechnology and the Human Good*. Washington, DC: Georgetown University Press, 2007.

Waters, Brent. *This Mortal Flesh: Incarnation and Bioethics*. Grand Rapids, MI: Brazos, 2009.

Conclusion

Preserving Our Humanity
in a Biotech Century

I n previous chapters we have dealt with the taking of life, as in abortion and euthanasia; the making of life, manifested as embryos made in the laboratory through IVF as well as cloning; and what some have referred to as "remaking" or "faking" life, from human-animal hybrids to planned full-sized avatars that will have uploaded human consciousness without human senescence. Some of these have been occurring for years; others are still being translated from the drawing board to actual experience. More, much more, is being imagined.

Now is the time to consider how we will approach the various conundra that come our way. Open embrace of all change is not the way of wisdom. Rather, we need to consider our ways, draw the trajectories of proposed changes, and, to the best of our abilities, understand the effects of such proposals not only in our own time but for the generations to come.

Case: The Human Commodity Fair:
With Apologies to John Bunyan

In my dream I heard faint but festive music. As I neared, I could make out the bouncing notes of the calliope wafting through the air: dat, dat, dah-da dah-da, dat, dat, dah-da. It was a fair! From a distance I could see hoards of people crowding the midway. Yet the sights, sounds, and even the smells of this fair were different from those I'd experienced in the past. No cotton candy, Cracker Jacks, or corn dogs. Nor did I find a single carney game with its iconic giant stuffed teddy bear, which no one ever won. No, this fair was different.

I approached a kiosk that advertised the sale of human organs. The special that day was on kidneys. Surely this was a nightmare. No one would put human tissues and organs on the auction block. Yet here they were. And even fetal body parts were on offer. Fetal tissues for sale: how macabre. The sales representative was dressed smartly. He spoke in calm and soothing tones as he handed me a price sheet, reminding me, "You never know when you might need these."

One woman gazed longingly at the merchandise. She had parked a pram holding a baby to the side, and her small daughter stood nearby. The woman, obviously pregnant, was looking at the blown glass vials that stored the elixir of life: stem cells of all varieties. Personal bar code stamps were available for each family member. Entire embryos were here also—no doubt surplus ones from the fertility clinics. Oh, and there was a "Build a Boy/Build a Girl" machine! Why hadn't she thought of that earlier? A little girl with musical talents would be such a nice addition to the family! Perhaps the next time, if there was a next time. The government, it seems, had placed a limit on the number of offspring in each family.

The next kiosk rested under an elaborate awning. Above was the banner: "*C'est Moi* Boutique." Summoning my high school French, I came to understand this was a designer boutique of a strange sort. "It Is I" was not selling cosmetics, hair care products, or imported fabrics. It was offering the ultimate in self-design. However, just as in the finest fashion boutiques, there was a small library of catalogues with jaw-dropping choices. "DIY Genome" offered the latest in somatic cell reengineering. "Need a few extra IQ points? Never been easier!" "Want to keep those unwanted pounds off forever? Tweak your metabolism through genetic enhancement." "Keep forgetting where you left your keys? Get a memory boost through genetics!" "Not satisfied with nature's roll of the genetic dice? Let us help!" Bold promises indeed. And there, just in the corner of one of the bookshelves, I saw it, a goose. And just where you thought it would be, a golden egg. What a fitting symbol. *What's next*, I asked myself, *a fountain of youth?*

I saw a couple holding hands, peering wistfully into the boutique, wondering if these enhancements could be theirs. But, judging from the price tag on some of the services, only the rich could access the Gucci equivalent of self-design. After all, one of the keys to the marketplace is creating a felt need that makes people reach deep in their pockets to enjoy the pleasures of the rich and famous. Manipulating one's genome makes designer handbags look like plastic bags at a big-box superstore.

I watched carefully the people coming into the last booth. Their faces were amazingly beautiful. Their bodies were toned and many tanned but none overmuch. Their teeth were pearly white and perfectly even. No noticeable scars or wrinkles marked their faces. Even those with white hair—which were few, indeed—had no sagging chins. I walked toward a man about my own age, as he walked toward the woman at the counter. He didn't slow his pace as I approached. We were about two feet apart, and then there was no intervening space. Our bodies collided, but I felt no pain. The collision, if one could call it that, lasted a second or less. He didn't stop; he didn't have to. He passed right through me, ephemeral and ghostly.

Then I asked myself, *Could this truly be the future of our humanity? What is the cost of turning our humanity into a commodity to be bought, manipulated, augmented, and sold?* The answer seemed so clear to me in my dream. The cost of commodifying our humanity is losing our humanity.

And with that realization I awakened in a cold sweat.

John Bunyan's famous allegory *Pilgrim's Progress* includes a similar scene as the one described here. He visited a place he called Vanity Fair where he observed the wild abandon of human desire and the temptation of the world, the flesh, and the devil.

Clearly human desire is the common factor in both Vanity Fair and the Human Commodity Fair. Human beings are desiring beings. As Saint Augustine famously argued, our desires may either be properly ordered or damningly disordered. And to complicate matters, because of our fallenness, ordered desires have become disordered. So the proper desire to love one's neighbor can become disordered if love turns to lust and if the neighbor is already married. Similarly, the ordered desire to employ technology for human good can become disordered when it becomes a desire to alter our humanity. Then the technologist becomes the technology!

Emerging developments in biomedicine and biotechnology tempt us to redefine what it means to be human. Life-extension technologies fight against aging. Artificial intelligence wars against failing memories. Robotics replicate the organic body. And that's not all. As Oxford scientist Baroness Susan Greenfield declares:

> In ways, then, that we could never have imagined, the technologies of the twenty-first century are challenging the most basic compartments by which we have made sense of our environment, and lived as individuals within it. Information technology, nanotechnology, and biotechnology are blurring or even breaching every dichotomy that has until now transcended any particular culture, and held firm for every human society: the real versus the unreal; the old versus the young; the self versus the outside world.[20]

Medicine is one of the arenas where the revolution is occurring. As we have seen in previous chapters, although medicine is a human good, it may not be good in every way. When used to prevent illness, heal, cure, or improve the quality of life of those who are suffering, all things being equal, medicine is good. In so far as any practices of medicine end up dehumanizing patients, those practices should be resisted. Moreover, we should (re)discover ways to preserve our humanity in the face of attempts—whether intentional or not—to alter it. In this final section we want to offer a litany of ways we may protect and cultivate our humanity.

Moral Medicine

The relationship of a physician with his or her patient is an inherently moral relationship. When a patient, typically with some disease, presents to a doctor, one who typically has years of clinical

---

[20] Susan Greenfield, *ID: The Quest for Identity in the 21st Century* (London: Hodder & Stoughton, 2011), 12.

training and experience, an ethical context is created in which the physician brings the best of his or her skills—and his or her humanity—to serve another person's well-being. The disequilibrium created by the patient's disease and the physician's skills is laden with moral obligations. The physician has committed herself and her training to the patient's well-being. She has promised never to harm the patient. This is why the Hippocratic physician covenanted to "prescribe regimens for the good of my patients . . . and never to harm anyone." Through the course of the physician's training, the mantra, "for the good of my patients," should have become far more than a slogan: it should have become the physician's way of inhabiting the world.

European phenomenologist Pierre Bourdieu suggests that we do not inhabit the world as pure thinking things, as pure rationalists, but as actors in the world.[21] That is to say, we do not "decide" our way through each day, carefully calculating every move as if we were computers made of meat. Rather, we embody a *habitus*—a complex of inclinations and dispositions—that, upon reflection, help us understand that we are primarily "doers" who are acting on the world rather than "thinkers" who perchance do things. Moreover, most of us function within a community of practice—whether bankers, lawyers, physicians, bricklayers, chefs, educators; we embody the habitus of the community of which we are members.

Bourdieu's theory of the "logic of practice" and the place of *habitus* has applications not only to the skills of medicine but to the ethics of medicine more broadly. Every medical student knows the refrain, "watch one, do one, teach one," where "one" refers to some procedure. Students who have studied anatomy and physiology (and a host of other subjects) are to watch a procedure, like putting in an arterial line. Next they are to place an arterial line in a patient successfully. Then they are (presumably) prepared to teach another student how to do the same.

Medical training is meant to help a medical student or resident develop good clinical skills as a habit. Especially in acute situations (e.g., emergency medicine and surgery), a physician does not have the luxury of consulting a medical textbook before intubating a patient or doing CPR. Those practices must become what

---

[21] Pierre Bourdieu, *The Logic of Practice* (Stanford, CA: Stanford University Press, 1992).

we describe as "second nature." Not only do physicians learn to embody the habits of good or bad clinical skills, however; they also learn to embody professional virtues or vices. Hopefully they learn from their mentors what a "good doctor" looks like and how that good doctor treats patients. That "great bedside manner" patients often discuss among themselves need not only imply a pleasing etiquette. It may be, even more importantly, an apt description of a virtuous physician. It may well describe a state of affairs in which the disequilibrium—that imbalance of power between a physician and patient—is slowly eroded by a sense of confidence and comfort in a doctor who takes his or her moral obligations seriously—a person who is habituated "to prescribe regimens for the good of my patients . . . and never to harm."

The *moral* life of a virtuous physician, nurse, or pharmacist is not characterized primarily by a kind of ethical cleverness that enables him or her to reason through the next case presented in ethics grand rounds, or a moral ingenuity that finds ethical loopholes, but by a moral *habitus* that shapes every relationship, especially relationships with patients.

Keeping human medicine human is no easy task in today's hypertechnologized, politically polarized, and superbureaucratized health-care setting. Physicians must continually fight to spend more than five to ten minutes with a patient. In the hallway of the hospital, they must remind themselves constantly that in the room they are about to enter is not a problem to be solved or a disease to be cured but a living human being with a name, a family, and hopes and dreams. The pressure to objectify the person is enormous. And it must be resisted at every turn.

Communities of Care

The acids of contemporary culture have eroded communities of care. For millennia illness and death occurred in the context of caring families, churches, synagogues, and other caring communities. Today the ill are consigned more often than not to the sanitized environment of a hospital.

A preponderance of those patients die after decisions have been made to forgo life-prolonging treatment when only comfort care is required. Not only is this a huge burden on an already stressed health-care system, but it can also rob dying patients of the solace of family, friends, and fellow believers. Especially when there is no cure, there should be care.

In Genesis 2:15 we read that "the LORD God took the man and placed him in the garden of Eden to work it and watch over it." Care for God's creation was one of the principal responsibilities given to Adam, Eve, and their progeny from the beginning. If earth care is important, how much more important is care for those who are made in God's image. People of faith must recover an ethic of care.

Churches are finding a number of ways to become better communities of care. Many churches have found that participating in a pregnancy care center is an effective way to help women find alternatives to abortion. CareNet, a network of more than 1,100 pregnancy care centers, has been an important ingredient in lowering abortion rates in the United States. Pregnancy care centers may offer free pregnancy tests, ultrasounds, information about fetal development, parenting classes, and material assistance to empower women to choose life. As an umbrella organization, CareNet seeks to promote, prepare, and plant pregnancy centers across North America.

Parish nursing care is another example of how churches can help contribute to communities of care. Also known as Faith Community Nursing, trained nurses are employed by churches or groups of churches to provide a variety of health-care services in the community. There are approximately 15,000 parish nurses in the United States of which about 35 percent are compensated for their ministry. According to the Canadian Association for Parish Nursing, faith community nurses may serve in the following roles:

H—Health advisor
E—Educator on health issues
A—Advocate/resource person
L—Liaison to faith & community resources
T—Teacher of volunteers & developer of support groups
H—Healer of body, mind, spirit, and community[22]

Interfaith clinics provide care for many people. For instance, the Church Health Center in Memphis, Tennessee, is committed to "reclaiming the Church's biblical commitment to care for our

---

[22] *Parish Nursing Fact Sheet*, accessed March 18, 2014, http://www.valleyhealthlink.com/upload/docs/Parish%20Nursing%20Fact%20Sheet.pdf.

bodies and our spirits." For more than twenty-five years the Church Health Center has provided a health clinic for uninsured children and adults, including dental and eye-care services, social services, and counseling. They even partner with their farmers to host a community farmer's market complete with a "nutrition kitchen" to teach people how to prepare food more healthily.

In his carefully argued volume *The Anticipatory Corpse: Medicine, Power, and Care for the Dying,* physician-ethicist Jeffrey Bishop modestly offers a radical proposal for reforming medicine. Bishop argues for what he calls an "embodied holism" in medicine where patients and their bodies are not dissected from their lives, communities, projects, health, or illness. He calls all of us—physician or not—to rehabilitate the theology of "being-there-with-others and suffering-there-with."[23] The entailments of doing so would profoundly change the way we care for the dying.

Increasingly churches and faith community groups have begun hospice and palliative care programs as an expression of this kind of embodied holism. One of the most inspiring stories is from Our Lady of Perpetual Care Cancer Home in Atlanta, Georgia. Founded in 1939 by the Hawthorne Dominican Sisters, Our Lady of Perpetual Care accepts no remuneration from the patients or their families, even though they may be able to contribute something. By their own testimony, the Sisters place their trust in the loving providence of God, and he has never failed. Donations from groups and individuals have provided the necessary funds to provide end-of-life care for patients at the home. Church-based hospice will become crucial in staving off the juggernaut of assisted-suicide in a health-care system where it's much cheaper to help people end their lives than it is to help them live their lives until the end.

Humanity Over Efficiency

More often than not, the reason we adopt new technologies is because they allow us to do more work in less time. Technology, whether information technology or biotechnology, promises us two things: efficiency and power. These are often good things. But when we allow efficiency and power to be our most important values, we diminish our humanity.

[23] Jeffrey P. Bishop, *The Anticipatory Corpse: Medicine, Power, and the Care of the Dying* (South Bend, IN: University of Notre Dame Press, 2011), 295–309.

For instance, we are learning that the power and efficiency of "fast food" are killing us. Fewer and fewer Americans actually sit down to eat a meal with others that is prepared by someone they know from ingredients grown by people they know. We grab something from a drive-through prepared on an industrial food line by strangers with products grown by faceless people on the other side of the country. Sure it's powerful. Sure it's efficient. But it's also inhuman. Human beings are the only creatures on the face of the earth who eat not just to consume calories but as a deeply social activity.

In his luminous work, *The Hungry Soul*, University of Chicago professor Leon Kass, MD, declares, "Hunger hungers for more than fuel, just as eros longs for more than 'having sex.' The materialistic view of life, though it may help put bread on the table, cannot help us understand what it means to eat."[24] When we rob ourselves of all opportunities to find social meaning in social eating, we rob ourselves of our humanity.

> In an effort to increase power and efficiency and in the name of so-called liberation and sophistication, we have accepted and even encouraged the demystification of life and the world. . . . Strangely, our telescopes and microscopes (and the technologies that accompany them) have destroyed our perspective on the naturally visible world of ordinary experience. Like the one-eyed Cyclops, we too still eat when hungry but no longer know what it means.[25]

So we need to develop and cultivate practices that celebrate our humanity. Invariably those practices that attend to most of our embodied humanity—exercise, stress reduction, family life, spiritual formation, community involvement, and so forth—end up being life prolonging and promote overall well-being.

Hope Over Hopelessness

In January 2010, Charlotte Raven, a journalist from the UK penned a powerful piece asking the question, "Should I take my own life?" At forty years of age, with an eighteen-month-old daughter, she

---

[24] Leon R. Kass, *The Hungry Soul: Eating and the Perfecting of Our Nature* (Chicago: University of Chicago Press, 1999), 230.
[25] Ibid., 230–31.

had received most unwelcome news. She had tested positive for Huntington's Disease (HD). She proceeded to investigate various methods of being in control in her dying. She penned her reasons:

> My mind clicked into gear, issuing bullet points to back up the case for self-destruction:
>
> - If my cat had HD, I wouldn't make it carry on, but would get the vet to put it out of its misery.
> - Without autonomy and the capacity for self-determination, life is meaningless. Merely existing isn't enough.
> - Dependency is degrading.
> - Suffering is pointless. The religionists' belief that it is spiritually instructive, and therefore an essential part of life, is dangerous and reactionary.[26]

She began composing a letter to her daughter, and the family enjoyed some special days out. Ms. Raven read everything she could find about HD and was particularly intrigued by the account of a community of people with HD in Venezuela. She visited there and was at first offended by a number of things she saw, like the uniforms printed with teddy bears hugging rabbits. But that changed. She had expected a boring mealtime, but since difficulty swallowing is a prominent feature of the disease, eating with HD is a battle. She found herself inwardly cheering when a man with HD finished his meal unscathed. She saw raw grief in a woman patient whose son would not be able to visit that weekend. More than once the nurse hugged the patient for a long time in recognition of the painful loss she was experiencing. Ms. Raven found more:

> I, too, longed for a hug. One of the carers, Margarita Parra, obliged. In her arms, I feel like a rabbit being hugged by a teddy bear. I forget all my questions, which feels like a blessing.
>
> Earlier in the day, Nurse Guerrero had told me I should listen to what people were saying, rather than assume I knew. I felt annoyed until I realised that that is what I had been doing with the patients, assuming their lives were

---

[26] Charlotte Raven, "Charlotte Raven: Should I Take My Own Life?" *The Guardian*, January 15, 2012, accessed July 14, 2013, http://www.guardian.co.uk/society/2010/jan/16/charlotte-raven-should-i-take-my-own-life.

meaningless. I'd been doing the same thing with myself, too, assuming I knew what I would want without listening. In Margarita's arms, I tuned into my being. I became aware of my self-consciousness about when would be the right time to pull away from the embrace, my anxiety about the photographer hovering nearby, my grief for the future, and my fear that I will end up like Luzmila, yearning for my children with no way of holding their attention.

Registering the discomfort of existence, I felt a great wave of self-pity, the first since my diagnosis. I felt worthy of being cherished and knew I'd do whatever it took to survive.

Back home, I told my husband he was right. The case for carrying on can't be argued. Suicide is rhetoric. Life is life.[27]

In the midst of what many would consider hopelessness, Ms. Raven found the answers for which she was looking. Mother and daughter, along with husband and father, have the hope of spending precious time together.

Humility Over Hubris

Finally, to thrive in the remainder of the twenty-first century, we must cultivate humility both as individuals and as a species. Otherwise our hubris may be our downfall. Recall from Genesis that after the flood as people multiplied they grew in their independence from the Lord. In Genesis 11:4 we read their expression of arrogance: "Come, let us build ourselves a city and a tower with its top in the sky. Let us make a name for ourselves." This was the so-called Tower of Babel. In his book, *Virtual Morality: Christian Ethics in the Computer Age*, Graham Houston points out that

excavated inscriptions indicate that these towers were meant to serve as stairways to heaven. They had a purely religious significance and had no practical use apart from religious ritual. According to the biblical narrative, they were symbolic of the desire to usurp the authority of the landlord. They were declarations of independence from

---

[27] Ibid.

the true God, yet also expressions of underlying religious needs.[28]

The technology, in this case a tower, was symbolic of human rebellion against the God who made them. The problem, as Calvin College political scientist Stephen Monsma has said, is that "when human beings set themselves up as masters of their fate, they set themselves up not for an ascent to freedom, as they imagine, but for a descent into slavery."[29] Today we find ourselves increasingly enslaved to our technologies. Instead of liberation, has our hubris resulted in our bondage?

Going Forward

What are Christians to do in face of these challenges? First, Christians must remain at the forefront of medicine. Nowhere are Christian compassion and care more needed and more evident than in human medicine. Providing healing medicine for someone who is suffering the unease of illness or injury is a powerful expression of neighbor love. Not only so, but Christians understand that caring for others is a means of serving their Lord. After all, Jesus taught his disciples that one day he would return and say to the faithful:

> "'For I was hungry and you gave Me something to eat;
> I was thirsty and you gave Me something to drink;
> I was a stranger and you took Me in;
> I was naked and you clothed Me;
> I was sick and you took care of Me;
> I was in prison and you visited Me.'
>
> "Then the righteous will answer Him, 'Lord, when did we see You hungry and feed You, or thirsty and give You something to drink? When did we see You a stranger and take You in, or without clothes and clothe You? When did we see You sick, or in prison, and visit You?'

---

[28] Graham Houston, *Virtual Morality: Christian Ethics in the Computer Age* (London: Apollos, 1998), 69.

[29] Stephen Monsma, *Responsible Technology: A Christian Perspective* (Grand Rapids, MI: Eerdmans, 1986), 25.

"And the King will answer them, 'I assure you: Whatever you did for one of the least of these brothers of Mine, you did for Me.'" (Matt 25:35–40)

As we have tried to show in this book, as we move farther away from the Judeo-Christian, Hippocratic virtues of medicine, the more difficult it will be to treat patients as persons made in God's image. In an age of skyrocketing health-care costs, we will be tempted increasingly to focus on the economics of medicine. Economic issues are important, of course, but we must not forget that human lives are at stake. Historically, Christians have been pioneers in alternative ways of providing care. The early Christian remedy for infanticide, for instance, was not first to petition Caesar to make it illegal but to establish orphanages to take in the little ones needing care. More recently, the hospice movement began when a Christian nurse, Dame Cicely Saunders, became concerned to offer better care for people at the end of life. With a growing euthanasia movement around the world, Christians must rise to the occasion to offer a compassionate alternative to ending a patient's life prematurely through a medicalized killing.

Finally, Christians can take a lead in shepherding biotechnologies in directions that truly serve human needs and not just pander to human desire. Technologically achieved immortality is neither possible nor desirable. God has already made us humans immortal. How we protect biomedicine and biotechnology from doing harm now is the urgent question. How we continue to develop them in ways that contribute robustly to human well-being is the challenge.

Additional Resources

Lawler, Peter Augustine. *Stuck with Virtue: The American Individual and Our Biotechnological Future.* Wilmington, DE: ISI Books, 2005.

Sandel, Michael J. *The Case Against Perfection: Ethics in the Age of Genetic Engineering.* Cambridge, MA, and London, England: The Belknap Press of Harvard University Press, 2007.

Swinton, John, and Brian Brock. *Theology, Disability and the New Genetics: Why Science Needs the Church.* London and New York: Continuum, 2007.

Name Index

Subject Index

A

abortion 47–48
  Abortion Act 61
  elective (voluntary) 48
  homicide 59
  Lord Ellenborough's Act 60
  Lord Lansdowne's Act 60
  medical 49
  Medical Act 60
  partial-birth 50
  surgical 49
  therapeutic 48
advance (treatment) directives 73
aging 179
Alan Guttmacher Institute 51
American Association of Pro-Life
      Obstetricians and Gynecol-
      ogists (AAPLOG) 52–53
American Congress of Obstetri-
      cians and Gynecologists
      (ACOG) 48–49, 51–53
Apostles' Creed 4, 135, 182
Arsenault, Trent 119
Ars Moriendi 69, 98–100
assisted reproductive technologies
      (ART) 110, 114, 117–18
avatar 169–70, 185

B

Bacon, Francis 99
Barnard, Christiaan 132
Benignus of Dijon 59
Bible
  canonical revelation 31
  community narrative 30
  law code 29–30
  universal principles 29
blastocyst 154
book
  of God 40
  of nature 40–41
Bostrom, Nick 174
Brown, Louise Joy 109–10, 152
Byrne, Paul 136

C

California 162
California Institute of Regenera-
      tive Medicine (CIRM) 162
Callistus 59
Cameron, Nigel 2, 154
capacity 90
CareNet 191
CaringBridge 130
cases
  Chad and Ryan 129–31
  Charles 67
  Debbie 9–10, 20

203